I would like to organize my entire book collection with the help of a librarian, following the standard book classification system, and make it a public library.

I would have liked to have seen Nirvana play live.

I would like to own the complete set of the <u>Oxford English Dictionary</u>, and Tipex out every single listed word.

I would like to cut all my T-shirts in half and have them stitched back together.

I would like to read every book I have bought.

I would like to make my own clothing.

I would like to drive an American muscle car across the United States, listening to my iPod on shuffle.

I would like to grow my own fruit and vegetables.

I would like to swim in the ocean every day.

I would like to meet Yoko Ono.

I would like to employ a professional proofreader to read all my sketchbooks and correct typographical errors.

I would like to sew zips on clothing in places where no zips are necessary.

I would like to create the smallest ton.

I would like to see a ton of feathers.

I would like to open a can of Piero Manzoni Merda.

I would like to add more paint to an original Picasso.

I would like to commission Sol LeWitt to make a wall drawing on a ceiling.

I would like to commission Tracy Emin to make a bed.

I would like to commission Erwin Wurm to write the lyrics for a Red Hot Chili Peppers song.

I would like to ask Paul McCartney to sing only John Lennon's solo songs.

I would like to ask the person who paints the walls of a gallery white to paint a canvas white and hang it on the gallery wall.

I would like to write down every single English word on a roll of paper.

I would like to commission Richard Prince to exhibit his joke paintings at a comedy club.

I would like to swim the English Channel.

I would like to own a John and Yoko "War is over" poster.

I would like to design a postage stamp with a drawing of an envelope on it.

I would like to take family snapshot photographs and apply the Image Bank copyright watermark in the bottom left corner.

I would like to stack five hundred reams of A5 copy paper in a stack the same proportions as a single pack.

I would like to take photographs of objects in pieces and make jigsaws whose pieces have the same shapes as the pieces in the photograph.

I like to wear clothes until the fabric wears out.

I like words that sound the same but have different meanings.

I like artworks that have conclusions.

I would like to record a CD with noise pollution, such as a jackhammer, a generator, and a burglar alarm.

I would like to perform a twenty-four-hour hug with Flávia in a public gallery.

I like both the words fluent and affluent.

I would like to make blank badges for people to wear over the logos and brand marks on clothing.

I would like to take an aspirin from Damien Hirst's medical cabinet.

I would like to hang Renaissance paintings in a gallery that smells of fresh oil paint.

I would like to attach a digital video camera to a powerful hand drill and press record while it spins round.

I would like to take photographs of the offices of curators and exhibit them in their offices.

I would like to take a photograph of the area behind a photograph hanging on the wall.

I would like to take a photograph of what was behind the scene that was photographed.

I would like to eat lots of garlic and then blow up balloons for a children's birthday party.

I would like to make an archetypal brown doormat on which the word welcome is replaced with the word puddle.

Daniel Eatock <u>Imprint</u>

Published by
Princeton Architectural Press
37 East Seventh Street
New York, New York 10003

For a free catalog of books, call 1.800.722.6657.
Visit our website at www.papress.com.

Organized and made by Daniel Eatock
Edited by Nicola Bednarek

Special thanks to: Nettie Aljian, Sara Bader,
Dorothy Ball, Janet Behning, Becca Casbon,
Penny (Yuen Pik) Chu, Russell Fernandez,
Pete Fitzpatrick, Wendy Fuller, Jan Haux,
Clare Jacobson, Aileen Kwun, Nancy Eklund Later,
Linda Lee, Laurie Manfra, Katharine Myers,
Lauren Nelson Packard, Jennifer Thompson,
Arnoud Verhaeghe, Paul Wagner, Joseph Weston,
and Deb Wood of Princeton Architectural Press
—Kevin C. Lippert, publisher

Library of Congress Cataloging-in-Publication Data
Eatock, Daniel, 1975–
  Daniel Eatock : imprint.
     p. cm.
  Includes index.
  ISBN 978-1-56898-788-0 (alk. paper)
1. Eatock, Daniel, 1975– —Themes, motives.
2. Graphic arts—England—History—20th century.
3. Graphic arts—England—History—21st century.
I. Title.
  NC999.4.E26A4 2008
  741.6092—dc22
                              2008001578

Contents

Accidents
Aerials
Alarm
Alignments
Archetypes
Arrangements
Associations
Attempts
Audio

Balance
Bed
Beliefs
Bikes
Billboards
Bins
Blank
Bleeds
Books
Bubble
Building Banners

Camera Straps
Camouflage
Car Batteries
Centered
Christmas Cards
Circles
Clichés
CMYK
Coincidence
Collaborations
Collections
Color
Commercial
Commissions
Composite
Composition
Confirmation
Connections
Construction
Contributions
Crop Circle

Dance
Dandruff
Dematerialization
Deviations
Digressions
Direct
Discoveries
Disruptions
DIY
Dogs
Double Takes
Drips

Echoes
Economy
Editions
Elephants
Embrace
Enthusiasm
Envelope
Exhibits
Extensions

Favorites
Fiats
Figure of Eights
Finds
Fingernails
Fingerprints
Fix
Flávia
Form
Frames
Friends
Function
Furniture

Gaps
Givens
Go
Gray
Greeting Cards

Hair
Hand Drawn Circles
Humble
Humor
Hole

Identities
Index
Ink
Instructions
Invention
Invitations
Ironies

Jewelry
Jigsaw
Jokes
Juxtapositions

Landmarks
Language
Lines
Lists
Logic
Logos
Loops
Lyrics

Maps
Maximums
Medium
Minimums
Miscommunication

No Smoking

Objectivity
Observations
Obvious
Open Systems

Pairs
Participation
Patterns
Pears
Photographs
Pie Charts
Pigeons
Plywood
Portraits
Postcards
Print
Process
Punch Lines

Questions
Questionnaires
Quick Thoughts

Races
Randomness
Readymade
Reams
Recommendations
Red
Reduction
Reflections
Repeats
Repetition
Resolve
Restrictions
Results
Reversals
Rotation
Rubber Stamps
Rules
Rumors

Sculptures
Seriality
Shifts
Similarities
Snapshots
Sound
Spectrum
Stacks
Statistics
Stickers
Stone
Stop
Subversions
Symmetry

Tape
Template
Thank You
Tick Boxes
Ties
Titles
Transitions
Treasure
Trees
Tools
Tube Ticket

Unrealized Ideas
Upside Down

Vandalism

Wait
Watch
Watercolor
Word Play
Wit

Tell me about this book.

This book contains 939 pictures; 202 Pictures of the Week, 161 Thank You Pictures e-mailed to me by people I have not met, and 84 pictures commissioned to document work.

How are the projects organized within the book?

The positioning of 90 percent of the material was informed by my Picture of the Week project, which spans the duration of nearly all other works featured. I started it in 2000, and it is still ongoing. The Pictures of the Week run in reverse chronology starting at the end of the book, with two images displayed in the bottom right corner of each spread. I positioned other works based on the Pictures of the Week, forming loose connections and associations through color, composition, titles, material, and format. I want the reader to make discoveries and associations while viewing the projects in the same way I do when creating them.

Is the structure of the book implicit for readers?

Only subliminally; it is backgrounded. Its main purpose is to provide a systematic framework, creating a seemingly random distribution of projects in an order that feels comfortable. As a result, the work feels semi-shuffled, and on each spread the reader can discover many coincidences and overlaps of ideas.

Will readers make the same connections between works as you make?

Some will, others won't. Some connections are simple and obvious, while others are more removed, more subjective. An early idea was to literally spell out the connections through captions, but I eventually removed them all apart from the one on page 102: "There is a red, a white, and a blue van on this spread to match the image below."

Why make a book?

I see the book as an extension of my practice, following the tradition of artists who make works using the format of books, such as Martin Kippenburger, Edward Ruscha, Hans-Peter Feldman, and Lawrence Weiner, among others.

Why design the book?

It is common for designers to design their own monographs. They feel they know their own work best and so are best equipped to present it. But I think that I have not designed this book but invented a system to organize projects and labored to produce the result.

What is your favorite book?

At age eighteen I discovered a book called Six Years: The Dematerialization of the Art Object by Lucy Lippard. To me this book reconfirmed that a concept can be equally as beautiful as its aesthetics. I was so excited that I read it too quickly, not fully appreciating its content, and had to read it again.

Following a Christmas tradition, my grandmother would ask my mother to buy a present for her to give to me on Christmas morning. My Mum later passed the task to me, so I bought a reissue of Six Years, which my grandmother then gave back to me on Christmas morning. I acted surprised, as promised, when unwrapping it. "Thank you, Grandma. A book on the dematerialization of the art object, just what I always wanted." She wrote a note on the inside front cover, and I treasure it over all other books.

Six Years made me realize that art and design were no longer disciplines that were motivated purely by aesthetics. I wanted to relate Lippard's ideas of dematerialization to graphic design, exploring objectivity, systems, and concepts, and remove as many aesthetic decisions from the design process as possible. I asked myself whether graphic design can be dematerialized, or whether the graphic can be informed by a concept.

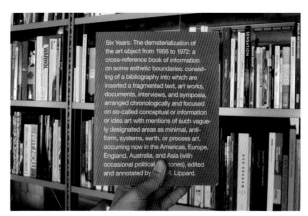

Favorite book

Hammertime
Thank You David Beesley

Four is the only number that when written out has the same number of letters as it represents.

You feature lots of works from other people in your book. Do you like to collaborate?

I like participatory projects. I like to make invitations and display the results. One of these projects is Thank You Pictures, which originally started as part of Picture of the Week, a single image displayed on my homepage that changes each week. I began Picture of the Week with an open invitation for others to contribute, and each week I would update the site and add the previous image to the archive.

After three years I decided to separate the contributions from my own pictures, resulting in two projects: Thank You Pictures, submissions e-mailed to me (usually from people I have never met) and Picture of the Week, my own pictures.

Both projects share the same concept, presenting incidents, alignments, coincidences, viewpoints, temporary situations, and other small things that often go unnoticed. The pictures are conceptual observations and not photography. The image is not as important as the content, and the title is as much a part of the work as the photograph.

These two projects have slowly evolved into a major part of my practice, infiltrating my everyday life and affecting my gaze and the way I appreciate the moment.

Red Poster Red Motorbike Red Car Red Jacket
Thank You Tunc Topcuoglu

Red Sign Red Sign Red Sign
Thank You Gavin Day

Stop Stop Stop
Picture of the Week

No Smoking Sign
Jeffery Vaska

Fork Lift Truck Lift
Picture of the Week

How is the book different from your website?

My website has evolved into an open space where I feel very comfortable publishing projects ranging from unfinished works and quick ideas, to commissioned works, invitations, and submissions from others. It acts almost like a box where the most recent project is at the top and the oldest one at the bottom. This chronology works well for the website, where an index list and exhibit area allow users to browse projects at will.

When making the book, I wanted to present a structure that was not about chronology. I wanted to show connections and recurring interests, almost forming a new work that consisted of previous works. In that sense the book is more complex than the website. It asks the reader not only to consider each separate project, but also the links and connections between works.

Did you read as a child?

No. I remember my mother taking me to the local library. I walked up and down each aisle and then told her, "There is nothing in here I want to read." I never got into reading, but as a very young kid I loved being read to before I went to sleep.

Were you creative as a child?

In primary school I was the best at drawing. My teacher, Mr. Bencley, called me Little Picasso, and I won all the drawing competitions and spent a lot of time making pictures. At high school, I was second best. Daniel Forster was much better. He could draw intuitively. I remember watching him draw from a plaster cast replica of Michelangelo's David and later, during a vacation we took together in the south of France, I saw him make amazing pen drawings on the beach.

I am competitive, and since I knew I could not compete with Dan's drawing ability, I understood that to be happy, I had to invent a creative way around the problem of making things look beautiful. So while Dan was drawing perfect renderings of the beach, I drew two straight lines on a page, dividing it into thirds. I wrote "sky" in the top third, "sea" in the second, and "sand" in the bottom third.

I realized in that instance that the craft and skill of drawing can be overcome with an idea. This simple realization has changed the way I approach almost everything I make. If something does not come naturally, I search out an alternative way to respond to the problem. There is a memorable scene in an Indiana Jones film: a skilled warrior wields two huge gleaming swords, elaborately swinging them around in circles, threatening to kill Indiana Jones. After this public display, Jones simply draws his gun, shoots him, and runs.

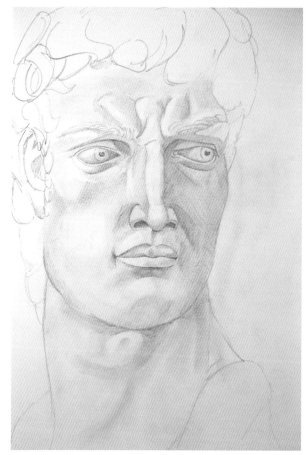

Pencil drawing by Daniel Forster

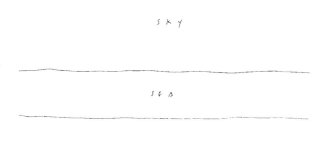

Remake of a pencil drawing I made when I was sixteen years old.

Six and twelve are the only numbers that when written out have half the amount of letters as the numbers they represent.

What were you like as a college student?

During my time at Ravensbourne College of Design and Communication in London I always arrived early for lectures and sat at the front. I tried hard to antagonize people with an unwavering commitment to my work. It felt punk rock to be the hardest working—a reversal of the cliché slacker student. I enjoyed provoking by being on time, having a well-thought-through solution to the brief that broke with the statuesque, and working when others were at parties.

Are you the same now?

I think I'm a bit less intense now. I still like to arrive on time and enjoy breaking with the statuesque, but feel more relaxed, and enjoy the things I do the more I do them.

What is your favorite color?

During my time at the Royal College of Art I adopted gray as my favorite color, because it felt neutral, a mid-way between black and white. I still like gray, but think it's a bit pathetic to claim it as a favorite color, as it lacks passion. So I embraced the most archetypal favorite color: bright red. It always goes well with black, white, or gray. Recently, I have been drawn to bright green, the exact opposite of bright red, its complimentary color. I often change my mind and do a complete reversal.

Small Medium Large
Picture of the Week

Cookbook Reflection

Canary Wharf
Thank You Anthony Burrill

Window Reflection
Picture of the Week

www.eatock.com

Through your website you seem to have built up a participatory community. Was this your intention?

The Thank You project has evolved naturally over four years. There is no explicit brief or list of criteria; people who see similar things want to share their discovery with the community. I also receive other submissions, accompaniments to works and proposals for projects. I like to embrace things that come my way.

A few years ago I started a project that more intentionally builds up a community when I invited people to replicate the structure and design of my website. My intention was to give emphasis to the sites' content by creating a network of people who use the same display. About two hundred people took me up on the invitation and built their own versions of a left-and-right-frame presentation platform, all linking to an index list of users.

I have since developed this project further in collaboration with designer and programmer Jeffery Vaska. We called the format Indexhibit, a new word that aptly describes the combination of index and exhibit. Jeffery created a web application (CMS) that allows others to create websites using the Indexhibit template. It was built with web standards in mind, no longer using frames, for instance, and allowing search engines and users alike easy access and indexing of work.

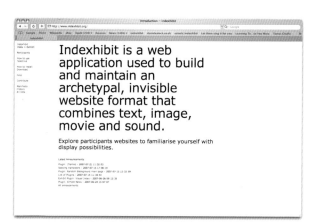

www.indexhibit.com

Why did you want to make a standard website format?

I felt that the web had so many options and standards were not embraced enough. I wanted to create a structure that could be navigated intuitively by all users, that was easy to maintain, and did not detract from the content. The more people use the format, the more recessive and archetypal it becomes, allowing the content to come to the forefront.

What is your fascination with archetypes?

Objects become archetypes when they function perfectly and make sense. I like generic things, mass-produced objects that are readily available. I would love to invent an archetype.

I compiled a list of archetypes as a manifesto to communicate the essence of Indexhibit.

Reusable Shopping Bag
Oxford English Dictionary
Swiss Army Knife
Sharpie
Rucksack
Zip
RGB Blue
Stapler
Roof Rack
Step Ladder
Tea Light Candles
Paperclip
Address Labels
Loofah
Map
Wire Coat Hanger
Tissue
Millimeter Graph Paper
Coffee
Tripod
Black-and-White Photocopy
DL Envelope
Plug Socket
Door Knob
Polypropylene Chair
Wax Crayons
Courier
Cork Wall Tiles
Cardboard
Ways of Seeing
Plaster
Sign Language
Allotments
Helix Ruler
Transit Van
Velcro
Park Bench
Dome Tent
Denim
T-Shirt
Post-it Note
Fixed-Wheel Bike
A4 Paper
CMYK
Havaianas
Glue Stick
A4 Sketchbook
A4 Ring Binder
Google
DIY
Rolodex
Gortex
Sellotape
Bic Biro

The trim size of this book matches the most archetypal paper size in Europe, A4. The size feels very familiar because most letters, utility bills, notepads, and diaries come in this size. For me this meant that while designing the book, I did not have to trim each page after printing it out. Pages can also be photocopied economically.

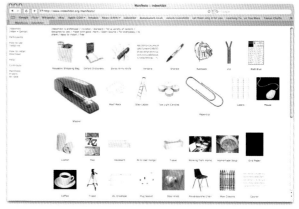
Indexhibit manifesto

Friends
Picture of the Week

Sitting Duck
Picture of the Week

Can you summarize in a couple of paragraphs the key moments that affected your practice?

At age eighteen I started at Ravensbourne College in London, studying communication design, and had an amazing first year being taught by Rupert Basset, Collin Maughan, and Geoff White. They gave me a rigorous back-to-basics Bauhaus Swiss modernist induction to design. I graduated in 1996 and went on to study for a further two years at London's Royal College of Art. A few months before graduation, Rick Poynor, one of my teachers there, suggested I look into an internship at the Walker Art Center in Minneapolis, Minnesota.

When I went to visit the Walker Art Center, I met the new design director, Andrew Blauvelt, and felt immediately inspired and committed to working there. I had an interview, got the job, and started in November 1998. I worked almost twenty-four hours a day, seven days a week, for just over a year. During this time I became friends with Sam Solhaug, who worked on the exhibition crew and with whom I collaborated on my first piece of furniture. In one of our conversations about art and design I mentioned an idea to cut an eight-by-four-foot sheet of one-inch plywood into one-inch strips, turn them all ninety degrees, and laminate them back together with the plies running vertically through the sheet. Sam suggested to also form legs from the plywood, transforming the idea from creating a plywood sheet turned inside out to producing a functional table based on the same concept. After stipulating that there should be no material waste, we independently drew identical cutting patterns and designed the same table. We worked for a few weeks after hours in the Walker's carpentry shop to build a prototype and decided to present it at the Milan Furniture Fair.

I returned to London at the end of 1999 and started teaching two-and-a-half days a week as the third-year graphic design tutor at Brighton University. I also found a studio space in Bethnal Green to pursue my own projects. In February 2000 Sam visited, and we spent three weeks working in Pentagram's carpentry shop (thank you Angus) to build a perfect 10.2 Multi Ply Coffee Table for the Milan Furniture Fair 2000. Together we decided to call our informal collaboration Foundation 33, inspired partly by a recent trip to Marfa, Texas, where the many Donald Judd buildings displayed "Judd Foundation" in bright red capital letters in their windows.

In Milan we met Lyn Winter, who for a 15 percent commission of sales offered to promote and find retail outlets for the 10.2 Multi Ply Coffee Table and future projects. Once back in London Lyn visited my studio and discovered that I was a jack-of-all-trades, not a furniture designer as she had first expected. So she introduced me to her friend Katie Hayes, who worked in the marketing department of Britain's Channel 4.

The first time I met Katie she was wearing a white jumper with two red cherries embroidered on each side. I showed her my projects, and a week later she invited me to pitch for the design of an identity for a new series of the megahit program Big Brother. After finding out there were another eight, much more established, design studios pitching for the job, I felt like the underdog.

I spent two weeks working for the pitch, at the end of which I asked my close friend Tim Evans for feedback. He said I had created something that I felt Channel 4 wanted, rather than following my own judgment. I knew he was right, so I started from scratch. In the following two days I made a very quick and direct ideas pitch, had a memorable meeting, and won the project.

What ideas did you present for the Big Brother pitch?

I had many ideas for each requirement of the program and presented about twenty concepts (but no logo). I proposed, for example, that the title sequence should be silent with a ten-second display of the archetypal broadcast countdown clock, and that billboards should show a picture of every applicant who wanted to appear on Big Brother. None of my ideas from the pitch were eventually used. In retrospect, the pitch was like a qualifying engine in a Formula 1 car: it's only good to secure poll position, but you have to turn the revs down for the race, or you will blow up. The challenge was to design a logo and Big Brother identity that could be applied to everything from the program title sequence to a baseball cap.

Eventually, I came up with a logo based on the simplified image of an eye that is camouflaged within a field of lines, which are derived from the horizontal interlacing lines of a television. Concealing the eye resulted in an identity that is staring back at the viewer, creating an optical sensation that affects the viewer's gaze. This manipulation echoes the main ethos of the show and reflects its Orwellian sense of concealment, typified by the surveillance cameras distributed around the Big Brother house.

What came next?

I transformed Foundation 33 practically overnight, from an informal collaborative project with Sam Solhaug to a business employing my friends Dan Forster and Tim Evans, who helped me deliver the biggest project of my life yet. Living and working in the same space, talking, and designing, we worked for almost twenty-four hours a day to produce the graphics for the second series of Big Brother. It was a success: the program had even more viewers and we had created, unknown at the time, an eye logo that would be used and updated each year for all subsequent series of the show. Thank you, Katie and Anna. I wish there were more brave people commissioning graphic design, and more organizations such as Channel 4 that embrace risk taking as part of their ethos.

Looking back now, I think the Big Brother project signaled the end of my collaborations with Sam. On retrospect I had mistakenly established a studio with a person I had only known for a couple of months on the basis of one collaborative project. From the beginning I was funding the studio by teaching, while Sam designed chairs and new Multi Ply tables. After a whirlwind four years there was a massive imbalance in the authorship of projects, resulting in arguments. Eventually, Foundation 33 ended by merging with the creative agency Boymeetsgirl to become the design wing of this new interdisciplinary company formed by Andy Law, Kate Stanners, and David Pemsel.

What happened to Boymeetsgirl?

It is not such an interesting story. I was the design director and continued making work for Channel 4. It was my first real insight into the world of advertising; until this point I had not realized that copywriters and art directors worked together in pairs. It felt like an outdated method of working. I was used to dabbling in everything, including language, invention, design, photography, making furniture, radio ads, teaching. I was a generalist—an amateur who was not constrained by disciplines.

After twelve months at Boymeetsgirl a big client did not renew its retainer, and very quickly the company spiraled out of control. I bailed out moments before the end, taking with me my large white table and my laptop. Thank you, Martin, for helping me carry the table down four flights of stairs. I was independent again and was excited to be free.

What was the first project you made after leaving Boymeetsgirl?

I simultaneously made a range of things, from a new Big Brother logo, to a Rirkrit Tiravanija book for the Serpentine Gallery, and a work called Tape Race for a small group show at the M+R Gallery in London.

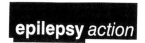

Channel 4 Television
124 Horseferry Road
London
SW1P 2TX

23 May 2006

Dear Sirs

Big Brother Newspaper Advertisements

I am writing on behalf of Epilepsy Action to express our concern at the full page Big Brother newspaper advertisements which ran in the national press last Thursday (May 18).

Having sought expert opinion on the ads, we have been informed that they are epileptogenic, i.e. they could possibly trigger a seizure for people with photosensitive epilepsy.

We would be obliged if you could advise us whether you plan to run any more of these, or similar ads, throughout the Big Brother season. If so, we would ask you to consider amending the design in the light of our findings.

Yours faithfully

Alison Knight
Press Officer

BRITISH EPILEPSY ASSOCIATION
New Anstey House, Gate Way Drive, Yeadon, Leeds LS19 7XY United Kingdom
Tel. 0113 210 8800 • Fax. 0113 391 0300 • Email epilepsy@epilepsy.org.uk • www.epilepsy.org.uk • Freephone Helpline 0808 800 5050
Patron: HRH The Duchess of Kent • President: Baroness Gould of Potternewton • Chief Executive: Philip Lee
A Company Limited by Guarantee (Registered in England No. 797997). Registered Charity in England (No. 234343). Registered Office as above

Letter regarding Big Brother press ads

White Sheep
Picture of the Week

Stalagmites & Stalactites
Picture of the Week

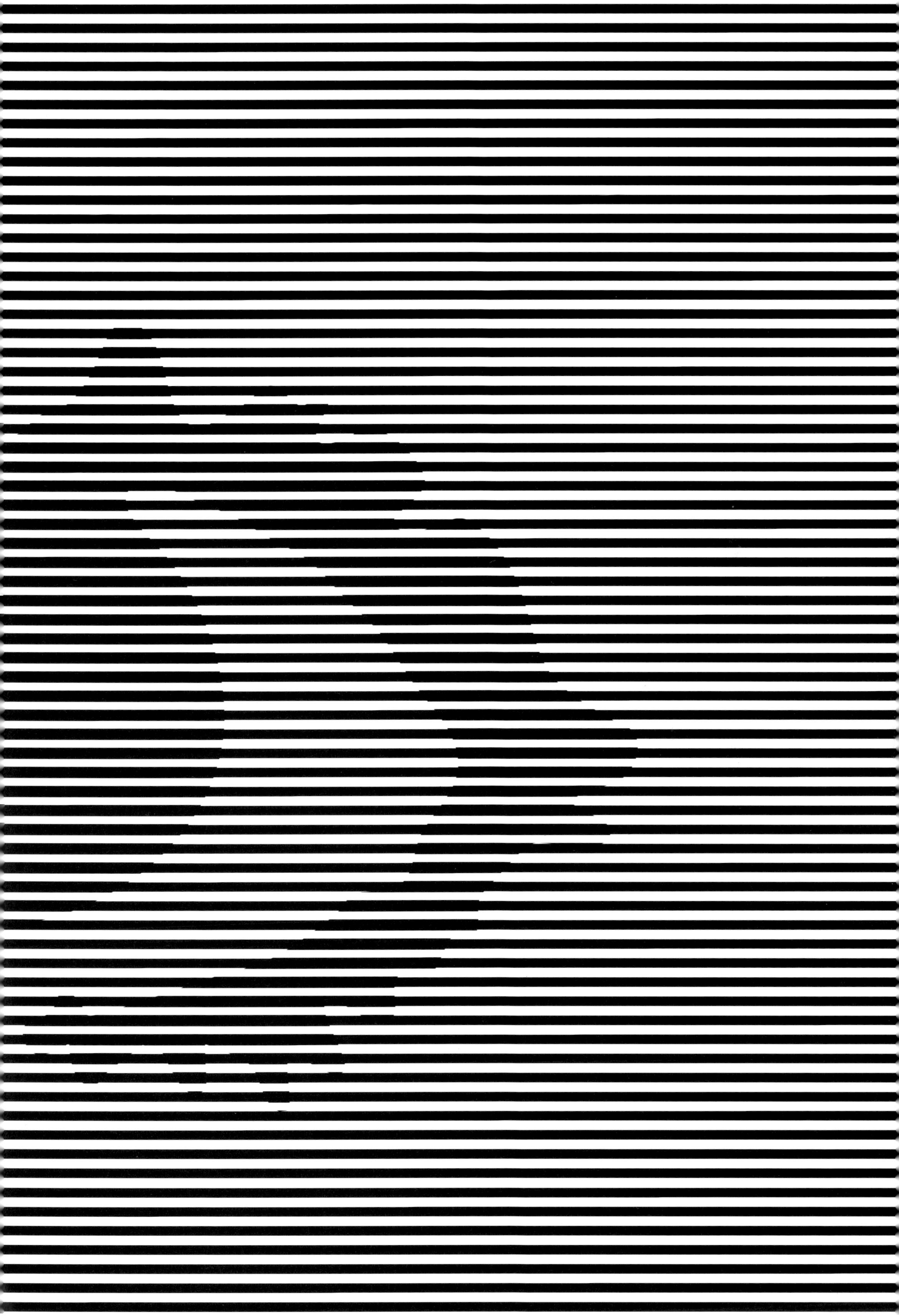

Do you stick to the brief when working on a commissioned project?

I have always been interested in embracing restrictions, in making the most out of what you have. I like challenges, such as "who can build the tallest structure out of ten sheets of A4 paper." I like set parameters to work within. In graphic design there is usually a defined medium or message, and it's the designer's role to push and challenge the restrictions to create something that communicates. My enjoyment comes at challenging the givens.

In Formula 1 races, teams are always on the edge of breaking the rules. The weight of the cars and drivers is so close to the allowed minimum that after each race on the slow-down lap, drivers drive on the outer edge of the circuit so that the hot sticky tires collect discarded tire rubber and gravel to add extra weight to the cars before they are weighed.

Have you ever stolen anything?

I stole a press image of Damien Hirst's diamond-encrusted skull For the Love of God and made a skull and crossbones, a pirate copy of the original work.

What is your favorite project?

This book.

To what questions would you like to know the answer?

What is the heaviest material in the world that is safe to sculpt with—i.e., non-radioactive—and what would the circumference be of a sphere using a ton of this material? Do Day-Glo colors have complimentary colors? Is it possible to make an audio recording of a sonic boom? Why do people smoke?

What things irritate you?

People who copy, smoking, dropping litter. The list goes on and on. Refer to the No Manifesto on page 58.

Who are the key people you work with when making big projects?

My colleagues change often. People float through the door, doing work placements, internships, or helping on specific projects. A few close friends who contributed significantly to important projects are Tim Evans, a friend from Ravensbourne College; Simon Jones, an architect and furniture designer; Flo Heiss, a friend from the Royal College of Art; Dan Forster, an old friend from high school; Jeffery Vaska, a designer and programmer based in Belgium; and Line Anderson, a close friend's sister.

No Smoking Sign
Justin Hutchison

No Smoking Sign
Henry Deighton (GCSE Student)

Echo
Picture of the Week

Driving Seat
Picture of the Week

The words "twenty minus five" have the same amount of letters as the result of this subtraction.

How controlling are you when working on projects?

My favorite works are the ones where control has been relinquished. I like setting up frameworks from which the project can then evolve. For instance, I am fascinated at just how many varieties of No Smoking signs exist. I am collecting as many versions as possible to add to my online No Smoking Sign Library (www.eatock.com/projects/no-smoking-sign-request/), where EPS files for each featured sign can be downloaded and used for free.

I invite everybody to draw a No Smoking sign to be added to the library. To contribute, e-mail a vector EPS graphic that fits within a one hundred millimeter square, using red and black colors only, to: daniel@eatock.com.

I was recently asked by Heidi Robertson, a second-year school teacher, if she could extend the No Smoking Sign project as a secondary school GCSE (General Certificate of Secondary Education) pictogram workshop. I was delighted and received some great results.

No Smoking Sign
Tom Crawshaw

No Smoking Sign
Carl Monte-D'Cruz

Are you against graphic design?

I never liked the term "graphic"; it suggests the surface, while I always prefer what is underneath the surface. I try to avoid subjective decision making, decoration, and unnecessary graphics. I like ideas and concepts that inform or dictate the aesthetic. I prefer the idea to stand out rather than the aesthetics, the content to stand out rather than its display.

Do you like miscommunication?

A few years ago I was featured in the New York Times. I was so excited that I asked my girlfriend Flávia, who was living in the States, to get me ten issues. She asked me why I wanted tennis shoes. I explained that I wanted to give them to friends and family. It took us both a few seconds to see the miscommunication.

Recently, my sister asked for a pineapple juice in a bar and was given a pint of apple juice. And when she was a kid, I heard her shout to my Mum and Dad to switch the dark off. Another time, when I was rebuilding some metal shelving, she asked if I was "mantleing" them, since I had previously dismantled them.

I really love miscommunication, or an opposite/sideways look at something.

How do you record ideas?

I feel that I always need to carry my digital camera with me, otherwise I will almost certainly miss a perfect Picture of the Week. One of the few times I forgot to take my camera, I saw a breakdown truck, broken down at the side of the road with smoke billowing out of the hood.

What tools do you use?

I once received an e-mail from a stranger who described my work as being made by a brain rather than a paint brush. The brain is the most democratic tool that all artists and designers share.

What is your obsession?

I like to draw circles freehand on A4 or A3 sheets of paper. At one time in my studio I had over twenty-five thousand sheets of paper in piles, each with a hand drawn circle. My favorite part was the join—how accurately the two end points meet. My obsession is to find sense in nonsense and nonsense in sense.

So you're obsessed by making circles?

I like circular ideas, like a dog chasing its own tail, or taking a photograph of the strap attached to your camera.

Occasionally, the camera strap sneaks into a picture by mistake, swinging innocently in front of the lens and distracting the attention from the intended subject. Camera Strap Photos, a project I started in 2004, on the other hand, are not mistakes. I invited people to intentionally place the straps in the picture. Each photograph presents an alternative: the backdrop to the camera strap now becomes a secondary subject.

What do you hope to design someday?

I hope to discover/invent/design an archetype— something that is so great that it becomes almost invisible, something that people use all over the world and take for granted.

What do you do when you're not working?

I go to lectures at the Tate Modern wearing my red jumper so I blend in with the completely red auditorium.

Camera Strap
Michael Place

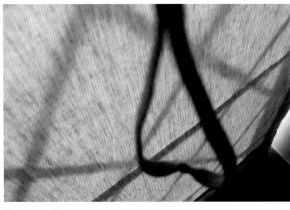

Camera Strap
Garus Booth

No Smoking Sign
Christian Eager

Portaloos
Picture of the Week

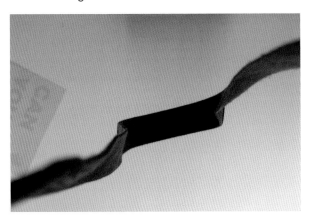

Camera Strap
Jack Crossing

Double Yellows
Picture of the Week

A Hans Ulrich Obrist Question: Do you have any unrealized projects?

Yes, I have two:

A CD is read from the inside of the disc to the outer edge. I would like to conceptually unravel this spiral and calculate the actual physical distance a CD can hold. Once the length of this unwound track has been determined, I would place beeps and voice recordings noting the distances the track has progressed—ten centimeters, one hundred centimeters, the length of an Olympic swimming pool, one mile, and so on.

The other unrealized project is called www.onemilescroll.com. I would create a website with a one-mile-long scroll, allowing the user to travel a physical distance in a virtual space. The scroll would start at the top and work its way to the bottom. The viewer would scroll down past the tallest objects displayed on the site first. Things featured would include the world's tallest buildings, a Jumbo wingspan, a stack of one million pound coins, a stack of one thousand Robin Day plastic chairs, the tallest human pyramid, the highest distance a human has thrown an object, the height of a giraffe, the length of an Andrex toilet roll, the tallest tree, and the lowest limbo. People would be invited to add new content.

Do you watch television?

It has been a long-standing joke with Channel 4 that I have never seen the programs I am designing for. Before I start working on a Channel 4 project, I receive tapes with past episodes so I can familiarize myself with them. Now I occasionally do watch TV, but the only thing I make an appointment to view is the Formula 1 grand prix on Sundays.

But I do remember two very memorable television programs from my childhood. The first one is Wide Awake Club, broadcast on Saturday mornings. The presenter Timmy Mallett played "Mallett's Mallet," a word association game in which contestants weren't allowed to pause, hesitate, or repeat a word or they would get bashed on the head with a large pink rubber mallet.

The second is Crackerjack, a British children's comedy BBC television series. The most interesting game of the show was a quiz called "Double or Drop." Children were picked from the audience to answer questions while holding on to an ever increasing pile of objects, winning prizes for a right answer and cabbages for a wrong one. They were out of the game if they dropped any of the items.

Tell me about your fascination for blank spaces.

I have an aversion to filling out forms, but I became fascinated with the idea of using instructions and blank spaces as an opportunity for people to complete my work. This goes back to my drawing of the beach: there is a lot of blank space asking the viewer to use his or her imagination. Not filling something in gives more potential to the reader to participate. I always prefer reading or listening to music to watching a film. I think that films give too much away—they are very descriptive, whereas reading or listening to music sets my imagination working.

Mosart
Thank You Helene Ryenbakken

No Smoking Sign
Robert Leguillon

Pick Ups Picked Up

Where and when were you born?

Bolton, England. 18 July 1975.

What was the fastest lap time around the Three Sisters Race Circuit?

50.24 seconds.

What gear ratio is your fixed-wheel bike?

42/22

Are there any questions that I have not asked that I should have asked?

Are you good at telling jokes? What is the best part of life? Who is your biggest inspiration? What was your most embarrassing moment? What was your first car? Who is your favorite Formula 1 driver? Do you have any secrets? What is your favorite fruit? How quickly can you recite the alphabet? If you could have a wish come true, what would you wish? Which musicians would you put together to form the ultimate band? Would you prefer to be run over by a steam roller or jump off the Empire State Building? Which is the fiercest animal? What is your favorite animal? Do you have any tattoos? What came first, the chicken or the egg? Who was faster, Ayrton Senner or Michael Schumacher? Would you take a time machine back in time or into the future?

Why are there pictures of car batteries randomly inserted in the book?

A flat car battery is a white elephant, both for the environment and the car owner. It is a very heavy, difficult object to dispose of. Some time ago I started noticing them everywhere. The abandoned batteries record the breakdown points of cars, and they're often found in cheaper parts of cities and towns, where cars are older and more prone to flat batteries. Because they are too heavy and large to collect, I started to document them in situ. I decided to abandon the car batteries throughout the book, in empty spaces.

British Isles
Thank You Shahnaz Ahmed

Taxi Ride
Picture of the Week

Off-Roader
Picture of the Week

Who would you like to thank and why?

Gina Bell for introducing me to Deb Wood and giving feedback on my early book proposal. Deb Wood for believing in the proposal and commissioning the book. Adrian Shaughnessy, Rick Poynor, Emily King and Jonathan Bell for feedback and help when first thinking about making this book. Rick Poynor for also introducing me to the Walker Art Center. Andrew Blauvelt for my first job and recently the chance to talk at the Walker Art Center. Rupert Basset, Collin Maughan, and Geoff White for a perfect indoctrination to design. Carlo Draisci for taking brilliant studio photographs on a seamless gray background. David Grandorge for super amazing large-format photos of billboards and for correcting the scans that Jon did badly. Sam Solhaug for making a good table. Dan Forster for drawing the perfect eye. Timothy Evans for the life-changing critique. Hanna Werning and Sara De Bondt for helping make things I could never have made on my own. Simon Jones for studio, home, kitchen, and bathroom. Arvid Wennel for moving from Sweden to start at Boymeetsgirl. Line Anderson for two great eyes. Katie Hayes for my biggest project to date and for taking a risk. Bill Griffin, Nick Stringer, Anna Skelton, Sophie Rouse, Pete Spires, Polly Cochrane, and other people from Channel 4 for causing trouble and being first. Kate Stanners, David Pemsel, and Andy Law for the introduction to the world of advertising. Ben Little for entrepreneurial brainstorming, excitement, and enthusiasm. My Mum for wit, curly hair, and love. My Dad for Le Mans trips, car building, kart racing, and love. My sister Charlotte for dancing, clowning, talking, and love. Flávia for not wearing perfume, appreciating the moment, staying stubborn, and love and happiness forever.

Who would you most like to interview?

Andy Warhol.

Why did you do an interview with yourself for your own book?

I wanted to include an informal, conversational addition to the works, providing references, memories, key stories, and thoughts that are of equal importance as the projects themselves, and I wanted to keep the content 100 percent homemade.

Interview by Daniel Eatock with Daniel Eatock

August 2007

Campbells Soup Can (Tomato), 1965
Whitechapel Road / Brady Street

Long johns and badminton shorts

Bin in Clerkenwell

I have an obsession with carefully turning all food products in my fridge and kitchen cupboards so the labels face the front, just like they are displayed on a supermarket shelf. I have more recently continued this fascination with Flávia's and my bathroom products. The single shelf that holds all our bathroom products is fairly deep, so that I placed products that are used often at the front, and products used less often in the back. The products became building blocks to form a composition of towers based on the inherent structure and organization of the seemingly random shelf display. It was not a practical display, however, and gradually, with use, the composition eroded and fell back into its natural order.

Artists and curators gerlach en koop invited me to show Bathroom Balance Composition as part of their group show Supermedium #14 in Rotterdam, Netherlands, in 2007. Upon their invitation I carefully packed up all our bathroom products and sent them FedEx to Rotterdam, along with a photograph showing the balanced composition. Thank you gerlach en koop for both the invitation and for carefully rebuilding the sculpture.

Double Yellows
Picture of the Week

Rubbish Rubbish Bins
Picture of the Week

Fingernails and toenails collected since 2000

This Way
Thank You David Parie

I like to grow my hair long and then shave it off. I don't like haircuts or hairstyles. I like both short, shaved hair and long, unkempt hair, and especially the in-between stage.

After washing my hair, I retrieve it from the plug hole, rinse it, and roll it into a ball. Each ball equals one hair wash; the large ones were made when my hair was long, the small ones when my hair was short.

Off-Roader
Picture of the Week

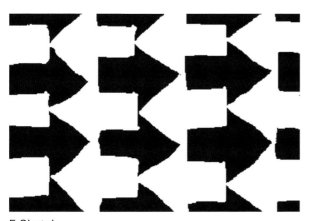

E Sketch
Natachia Pieterse

FedEx Deliveries
Picture of the Week

On my first day at Ravensbourne College, each student had to create a typographic self-portrait. Thirteen years later I can only remember one, made by Richard Holley. His response to this simple brief is one of the best pieces of graphic design I have ever seen. I have been bugging Richard for about a year, asking him to find his original portrait. He is still looking.

Holley Portrait
James Killcross

Holley Portrait Brief

I invite you to create your own version of the Holley portrait.

Write a short text about yourself. Include interests, likes, dislikes, and future plans. Using black ink, make a careful print of your thumb. Enlarge your black-and-white thumbprint to approximately the size of your face. On a clean sheet of A3 paper, handwrite your text following the contour lines of your thumbprint (with the help of tracing paper or thin copy paper). The final personal self-portrait is a combination of your words, your handwriting, and the pattern of your fingerprint.

Holley Portrait
Lori Flannigan

Very first gray hair

Holley Portrait
Silvia

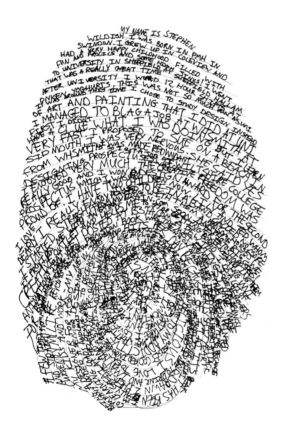

Holley Portrait
Stephen Wildish

Holley Portrait
Kieren Messenger

Similar Forms
Picture of the Week

No Grid
Picture of the Week

One Stone

I asked my Mum and Dad to take a set of bathroom scales with them when going for a walk in the countryside and to collect and weigh stones until they found one that weighed exactly one stone.

E Sketch
Dee Chettla

Flowers, 1964
New College Parade/Finchley Road

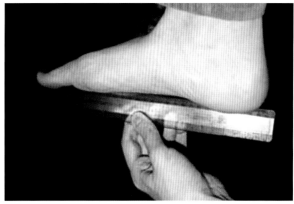

One Foot

I went to a restaurant with my Mum, Dad, and sister, and we started to roll balls of wax that we picked from the candle on the table. My Dad made the biggest one because he had the warmest hands.

Dear Daniel,

I saw the stone that weighs a stone on your website. I measured my foot, and it measured a foot (thirty centimeters).

Bye, Ben Harris

Similar Forms
Thank You Peter Ayres

Similar Forms
Picture of the Week

Flowers
Thank You Simon Jones

Flowers and Flowers for Sale
Picture of the Week

In 2007 design studio Glue Kit asked me to create and donate a T-Shirt design for their new charity initiative called Part Of It (partofit.org), to raise money for a charity of my choosing. I selected the International Dyslexic Foundation.

No Smoking Sign
Caroline Taylor

Bike Thieves
Thank You Ivar Martinsson

No Smoking Sign
Adam Jennings

Duchamp
Thank You Silvia Sfligiotti

Camouflage, 1987
Tower Bridge Road/Druid Street

Full Shopping Basket
Picture of the Week

Camouflage and Day-Glo
Picture of the Week

Frame with the same surface area as the A4 format it surrounds. Shown at 50 percent.

This frame was made in response to an invitation from Yuki at the Hat on Wall Gallery in London. The brief said, "Create something around an A4 sheet of paper / Keep A4 sheet space blank or white / The size of the object must be less than 10.5 centimeters from the A4 sheet, and if the object has depth it must be less than 3 centimeters deep / No limit to media or materials / The object should be able to be hung on the wall for an exhibition called: Frame of Mind, November 2005."

E Sketch
Jon Wicks

Frame
Thank You César Sesio

Frame
Thank You Graham Mansfield

Three New Bins and Three New Flags
Picture of the Week

Ed Gill, a friend of mine, spent one week in the woodwork shop at the Royal College of Art, working on two very large irregular hexagonal frames. The frames were intended for two informal quick drawings he had made with spray paint as part of a five-minute performance. After all his efforts the drawings did not fit his perfectly finished frames. At this stage, I would have recreated the drawings in a moment. Instead, Ed went back to the frame shop and started all over again.

Mask
Picture of the Week

Ream

Reconfigured Ream 1

Reconfigured Ream 2

Shopping
Picture of the Week

Green Carnoe
Picture of the Week

Dear Daniel

For my next exhibition in Paris, I am asking thirteen
artists and graphic designers to contribute by
designing announcements to the show in the form of
a poster. The show takes place in two galleries,
Atelier Cardenas Bellanger and Galerie de multiples,
so I'm asking each artist or graphic designer to
design two posters/invites (one for each venue).
The posters/invites will be sent out as invitations
and will also be the object of the exhibition: the
posters/invites to the first gallery will be displayed
in the second gallery, and the posters/invites to the
second gallery will be displayed in the first. I will
not show anything else than the thirteen posters/
invites in each gallery.

Jérôme Saint-Loubert Bié

Hello Jérôme,

For my poster designs I would like to propose two
composite posters, made by overprinting the other
twelve designs, thus forming the thirteenth design.

This would mean that as the first poster is printed,
extra copies would be printed. As the second poster
is printed, the extra copies would be overprinted
with the design of poster two. This would happen
twelve times altogether. I would not add any
additional information, so the production budget
would be used to extend the print run of the other
posters.

Dan

Overprinted Poster One

Overprinted Poster Two

French Rolls
Thank You Melvin Galapon

Atelier Cardenas Bellanger

Galerie de multiples

<u>Discarded Jigsaw</u>

<u>Chameleon</u>
Picture of the Week

For a show titled Deptford Design Challenge at the Royal Festival Hall in London in September 2007, thirty artists and designers were asked to re-use, re-interpret and re-appreciate a discarded object from the Deptford Thrift Market. I was given a two-thousand-piece jigsaw puzzle depicting a romanticized English country cottage.

<u>Camouflage & Cone</u>
Picture of the Week

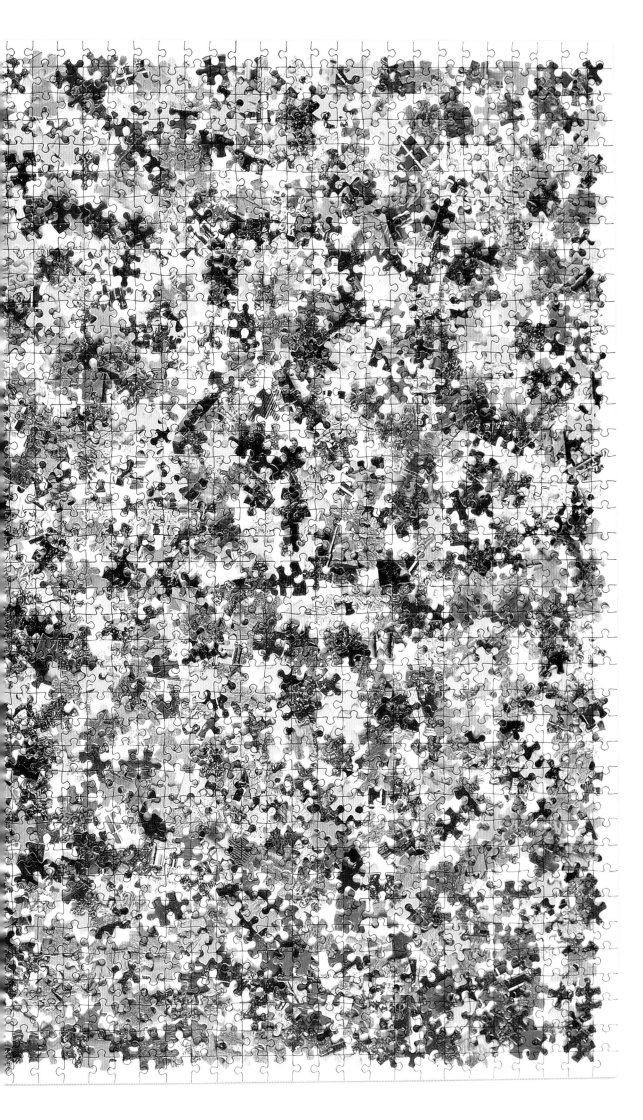

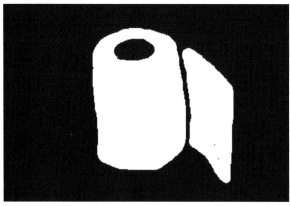

E Sketch
C. L.

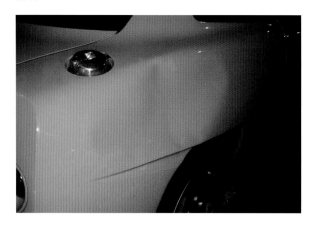 

An ongoing series of photographs of Fiat cars designed by Pininfarina. The undamaged Fiat displays a graphic slash as part of the car's styling above the wheel arch. Each photograph presents a car that has a second graphic mark as a result of an accident complementing the original slash.

Reconfigured Line

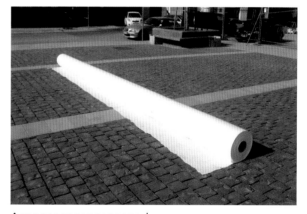

Aaaaaaaaaaaaaaaaaaandrex
Picture of the Week

Jigsaw

Bicycle Components
Picture of the Week

Rotated Grid

Headless in Gothenburg
Thank You James Payne and Nina Lundvall

All the people who have inspired me, whom I do not personally know, compiled from memory on 20 December 2001, São Paulo, Brazil

E Sketch
Joe Pinner

Every photograph of Flávia loose in a box frame

Painful
Thank You Thijs groot Wassink

Wheelchair
Picture of the Week

Grass Hedgehog
Thank You Ronan Dillon

Friends
Picture of the Week

This billboard was displayed in January, the coldest time of year in Great Britain. It acted both as a safety announcement for motorists, informing of the slippery road conditions, and as an advertisement for the start of a drama on Channel 4.

I have always liked things that have more than one purpose:

In one of the pavilions at the 2007 Documenta in Kassel, Germany I noticed a red letter F that was both a sign and a handle for a cupboard containing a fire hose. It was beautifully simple.

In Brazil, there is a very common soft cheese spread that comes packaged in a small drinking glass. Once the cheese is finished, the label on the container can easily be removed, and the glass looks like any other small drinking glass. I think this is the ultimate form of recycling— why aren't all glass jars designed with this dual purpose? My mother-in-law Liana always buys the same cheese so that her collection of glasses match. It's a win-win solution for everybody: the cheese manufacturer, the environment, and Liana.

Snowmobile

Defrost
Thank You Daniel Forster

Frose
Thank You Alistair Hall

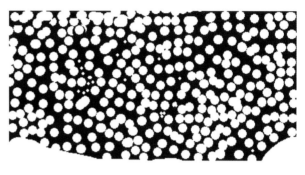

E Sketch
Andrew McCormack

Snow Parking
Thank You Jim Allen

Snow Delivery
Picture of the Week

Rubbish Snow
Thank You Rik Moran

Puncture Repair Pickup
Picture of the Week

I made two stickers to utilize the unused area on a Channel 4 print job. One of the stickers showed the image of a partly removed sticker (see page 198), the other one was this chewing gum sticker, which I stick underneath tables in cafes and friends' houses.

I often make use of the margins or other unused areas on the press sheets of commissioned projects. I like to work within the given constraints, such as the paper stock, colors, and dimensions.

Chewing Gum Sticker

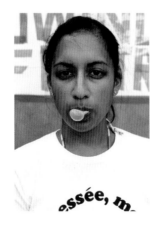

Logo for a music chart show on Channel Five

Sound in a Bubble

Pigeon-Made Donut
Picture of the Week

Spoiled Pigeons (they leave the crusts)
Thank You Krista van de Niet

Grumpy Old Man
Picture of the Week

Together with Flávia and my friends Tim and Naoko, I gave away bubble gum at a weekend street party, inviting passers-by to blow a bubble and take a self-portrait when the bubble was at its largest. It sounds easier than it was—people concentrated so much on blowing the bubble that they forgot to press the camera shutter release until the bubble had popped. I had imagined collecting many portraits of people with pink circular bubbles hiding their identities.

E Sketch
Nat Palit

Oxidation Painting, 1978
Eversholt Street

48

Superman, 1960
Harrington Square/Hampstead Road

Camera Strap
Darren Wong

Off-Roader
Picture of the Week

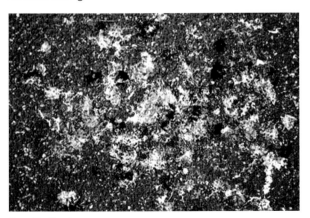

Poo Pollock
Thank You Myf Kemp

DIY DIY Shop
Picture of the Week

When the twenty-year anniversary of John Lennon's death approached, I started to think about his contribution to the world and tried to remember every single Beatles song title. I wondered how long a text would be that presented the complete song lyrics. Would it fit comfortably on an A4 page or a ninety-six-sheet billboard? The quantity of information was completely abstract.

In the following weeks I compiled all Beatles song lyrics in order of album release in one block of text. I wanted the text to be legible as individual words but also visible in its entirety as a unit. The result was the Untitled Beatles Poster, an A2 sheet containing over twenty-five thousand words. I still can start reading it at almost any point and recognize the song. I find it absolutely amazing that without even trying I memorized over twenty-five thousand words of information subconsciously.

The poster was printed on 8 December 2000, exactly twenty years after Lennon's assassination. Page 56 shows the second version, Untitled Beatles Poster Two, an A0 sheet with the lyrics listed in alphabetical order of song title. The second version contains only lyrics written by Lennon/McCartney, whereas the first poster includes lyrics to all songs the Beatles recorded but did not necessarily write.

Jumbled Sale
Thank You Arran Lidgett

Lyrics

I wonder how many song lyrics I know by heart, and how long a text would be that compiled them.

Ascending Wall Openings
Thank You Alex Bank

Fence and Deck
Picture of the Week

Sale Sale Sale Sale Sale Sale Sale Sale
Picture of the Week

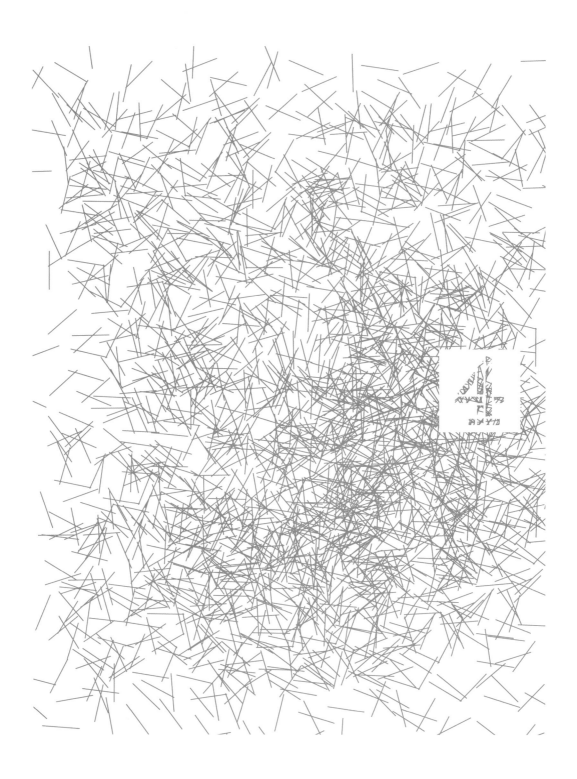

My design for the back page of Channel 4's 2004
Christmas magazine references the fallen pine
needles of dying Christmas trees. I am not religious
and find it weird that people celebrate the birth
of Jesus by sacrificing a living tree. It doesn't seem
so Christian to me to watch a dying tree lose its
needles. If you really want a pine tree, buy a live
tree and replant it outside after the holidays.

Rusty Christmas Tree
Thank You Mimi Bishop

The act of sending a card at Christmas time requires a huge amount of organization and planning. My Mum and Dad keep a Christmas card mailing list, which they update every year. In 1997 I created a card that displays all recipients' names in alphabetical order, including a section to accommodate names that may have been left off the list by mistake. Writing the card becomes a reflective process that exposes the network of recipients, many of whom know each other.

Trolley Park
Thank You Ollie Langridge

Limo
Picture of the Week

Acne
Thank You Joe Harries

Custom Car
Picture of the Week

Original drawing

In 2004 I bought a five-by-ten-foot sheet of birch plywood for a tabletop in my studio. After using it for a week, I decided that it was too large for my space, so I stood it upright resting against the wall. Lying on my futon on my studio floor, I mentally guesstimated that the sheet could be transformed into a bed base with just three saw cuts. An IKEA futon measures five by seven feet. After cutting three one-by-five-foot pieces from the sheet to form the H-shaped base, I was left with an economical one-foot-high bed base on which the five-by-seven-foot top rested with an overhang of one foot at both ends, accommodating the futon exactly.

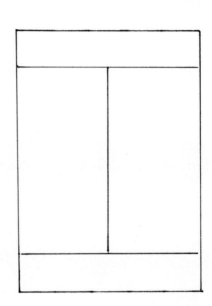

Cutting plan

1. Three one-by-five-foot pieces

2. H-shaped base using three one-by-five-foot pieces

3. Completed bed

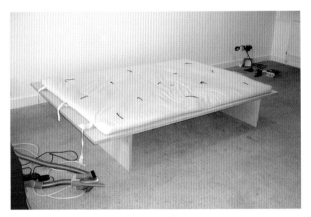

4. Completed bed with IKEA futon

5. Ready for sleep

<u>Makeshift Wrestling Ring</u>
Thank You David Oscroft

<u>Young Budget Hostel</u>
Thank You Peter Stadden

<u>Reflection</u>
Picture of the Week

<u>Stand-in Cones</u>
Picture of the Week

Visiting my Mum and Dad at Easter, I discovered that my Mum had peeled off all stickers from the fruits in the fruit bowl and stuck them on a single clementine. She didn't like the fruits with stickers; she wanted unbranded fruits.

Organic Litter
Picture of the Week

Apple Mac logo with Apple Stickers
Thank You Mark Ferguson

Junk TV
Picture of the Week

No dropping litter
No urban 4x4s
No blocking cycle lanes
No religion
No junk e-mail
No telemarketing
No smoking
No ignoring people
No perfume
No dumb advertising
No drunk driving
No copying ideas
No objectification of women in advertising
No dumping car batteries
No free pitches
No sugar in coffee
No hitting
No leaving the tap running while cleaning
  your teeth
No leaving the TV on stand-by
No freewheeling
No fast food
No illegally dumping waste
No poker websites
No leaving the fridge door open
No bank charges
No fee for withdrawing money from cash machines
No bending the corner of a page in a book as a
  page marker
No skirting boards
No down lighters
No carpet
No automatic cars
No being late
No replying to group e-mails
No paying rent
No hiding gray hair
No secrets
No milk
No fashion trainers
No war
No gold jewelry
No diamonds
No guns
No cycling fast past pedestrians on canal tow paths
No vicious dogs without leads
No spitting
No spitting chewing gum on the street
No adding service charge and also leaving room
  for a gratuity on the bill
No driving slow in the fast lane
No guarding an empty table in a café while your
  partner stands in line
No eating too much
No chewing the ends of pencils and pens
No leaving the washing up after dinner
No serifs
No spray mount
No direct mail marketing
No decoration
No fireworks sold to children
No coffee before bed
No instant coffee
No performance-enhancing drugs
No undertaking on motorways
No praying

No designing new buildings to look old
No retro design
No music packaging
No checking e-mails after 8 p.m.
No working on weekends
No Christmas decorations
No vacuum cleaner bags
No television on vacation
No sunbeds
No fake tan
No Flash websites
No celebrating Christmas in November
No Christmas shopping
No watching others do the work
No stepping back
No killing whales
No fur coats
No designer handbags
No talking on mobile phones while driving
No ghosts
No God
No UFOs
No packaging of fruit and vegetables
No overpackaging of general goods
No leaving the lights on while you're out
No microwave meals
No putting one's feet on the seats on public
  transport
No boiling more water than you need
No tattoos
No body piercings
No frozen food
No motorbikes and scooters in the cycle area at
  traffic lights
No back break on fixed-wheel bikes
No fashion accessories
No limousines and stretched Hummers
No pissing in the street
No gentlemen's clubs
No suicide
No monopolies
No hiding from the truth
No hunting animals for sport
No graffiti
No vandalism of private or public property
No overselling of seats on airplanes
No strong cleaning products in restaurants while
  diners are still eating
No long fingernails
No black tie dress code at formal events
No Christenings
No promising things you can't deliver
No piercing the ears of small children
No pushing in cues
No alcopops
No page three girls in daily newspapers
No Sunday newspaper advertising inserts
No standing on the left-hand side of an escalator
No overestimating on clients' print quantities, so
  they end up throwing old stock away
No taking the elevator when you can walk up
  the stairs
No

In 2006 John Walters, the editor of Eye magazine, invited me to talk at the first Eye magazine conference, called "Burning Issues," to talk about an issue I felt passionate about.

A couple of weeks prior to John's invitation I had made an A6 postcard that listed things I was against. I called it my No Manifesto. I hand the postcard to people I encounter who contravene one of the things listed in my manifesto. For the "Burning Issues" conference I expanded my No List and shouted it as loud as possible to the audience.

No Smoking Sign
Clara Lilley (GCSE Student)

No Smoking Sign
Jacob Mason (GCSE Student)

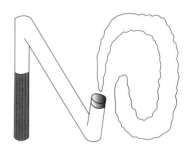

No Smoking Sign
Sheridan McWilliam (GCSE Student)

Kiss
Thank You Glen Birchall

Kiss
Picture of the Week

Not Here
Thank You Alex Rich

No Sign
Picture of the Week

Listen to your television

Carling Weekend Reading Festival	Mastercard MOBO Awards
Madonna Live: The Drowned World Tour	2001 MTV Europe Music Awards
Technics Mercury Music Prize	Smash Hits T4 Poll Winners Party
MTV Video Music Awards	Robbie Williams in Cologne
Ibiza TV	Pump Up The Volume

channel4.com/4music

In 2001 I invited my friend Flo Heiss to collaborate on an advertisement for Channel 4 that informed people of ten live music events. When brainstorming about the project, Flo picked up my TV, and I asked him to put it on his shoulder like a boom box. We walked outside, and I took a low-resolution shot on my new digital camera.

When I presented the image the next day to Katie Hayes at Channel 4, she loved it. I then spent a week trying to create a better version, commissioning a photographer to shoot a high-resolution picture, but the polished result did not work. The original informal ad captured the immediacy and spontaneity of the moment best. It just worked without trying. Eventually, the low-resolution JPEG file with its bad lighting was used.

Based on this ad, I also created a billboard for the MOBO (Music of Black Origin) Awards, which appropriated the vernacular of music bill posters. The pre-designed advertisement and the supplied MOBO logo were combined to create what appears to be a bill-postered billboard (see pages 62–63).

Fly Post-It is a city center version of the common desktop Post-it. It was created in 2003 for a street installation called Paper Jam, for which twenty designers explored the creative potential and reclaimed the often abused medium of fly posters. Pasted along its top edge, the majority of Fly Post-It hangs loose. The blank space encourages viewers to make public drawings, messages, memos, or notes.

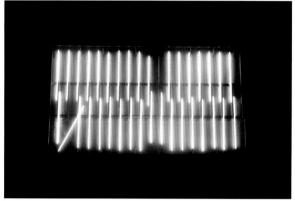

Seasonal Advertising
Thank You Marc Alcock

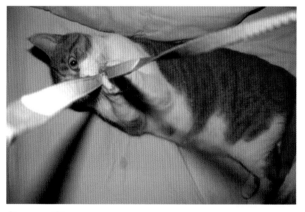

Camera Strap
Tom Balm

Backlit
Picture of the Week

Getting to Know Your Species
Thank You Esra Eren

Brave or Stupid
Picture of the Week

Complete roll of red duct tape...

...coiled around a one-inch-diameter steel table leg

In 2006 I was invited to create a seven-by-three-foot vertical banner using the form of a tree, which was exhibited in New York's Times Square as part of a group show called The Urban Forest Project. I selected Picture of the Week 41 2004 (shown on page 179), called Tottenham Court Road Deforestation, and rotated the image ninety degrees to give the tree a new life.

Barbershop Scaffolding
Thank You Melvin Galapon

Loop

Untitled Fences
Thank You Simon Jones

Chevron
Picture of the Week

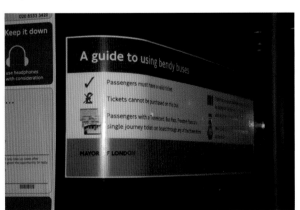

A Guide to Bendy Buses
Thank You Dan Duran

Stop Light
Picture of the Week

Bottle Top Wax Sugar Cube Sculptures

Volvic Mineral Water Color Painting

Five Coke Bottles, 1962
Elephant and Castle Northern Roundabout

Highland Spring Mineral Water Color Painting

Evian Mineral Water Color Painting

Buxton Mineral Water Color Painting

Under the Carpet
Picture of the Week

Airport Drought
Picture of the Week

Designers often have to work with logos that are difficult to position satisfactorily without interfering with the rest of the design. It seems like a universal battle between client and designer: the client always wants the logo to be bigger, whereas the designer makes it as small as possible and usually positions it in the bottom corner.

The Channel 4 logo style guide states that the logo has to be positioned at the far right and in the vertical center. Working on a billboard advertising the World Rally Championship 2002, I decided to embrace the restriction, starting with the mandatory logo correctly positioned according to the rules set forth in the style guide, and then repeating the logo many times to form a checkered pattern, the most recognizable icon of motor sport.

As well as informing the public about the World Rally Championship, this design also referenced the end of the race for motorists as they speed past.

In 2006 Sheridan Simove, a creative entrepreneur, commissioned me to design a logo for his new project www.winmytime.com, an auction site on which skills, advice, or even just a conversation can be bought and sold. It was a very enjoyable experience creating a logo for someone who is excited and passionate about both his own work and mine.

Visit the site, and buy and sell time. Help make it bigger than eBay!

Ten-Year Tour Guide Thank You Gift

In 1999 I was asked to design a thank you gift for Walker Art Center tour guides who had been working at the museum for ten years.

I created the ten-year gift watch, which features a carefully crafted sentence acknowledging that the recipient has been a tour guide for ten years. The sentence begins at twelve o'clock and wraps around the perimeter of the watch face so that the word "ten" is located in the number's normal position.

No Smoking Sign
Rola Al-Shwaikh (GCSE Student)

Three, Five to Three, Five past Three
Picture of the Week

Squat Stand Stretch
Picture of the Week

Silver birch

Rowan

Inspired by the reoriented image used for the Urban Forest Project banner, I started to photograph vandalized trees, rotating the camera so the tree stands vertical. The resulting alternative landscape gives the trees a new reality.

Tr ee
Thank You Cameron Wittig

No Smoking Sign
Andy

Common fir

No Smoking Sign
Denis Kovac

No Smoking Sherlock
Thank You Pierre Leguillon

No Bike, Wheels
Picture of the Week

End of Job
Thank You Anders Brasch-Willumsen

Cut
Picture of the Week

Silver birch

Birch

The way from my home to the high school I attended led past a roundabout, which the local council planted with about twenty young saplings in an effort to improve the urban landscape.
A few weeks later a mindless vandal had broken each tree at the point where it was supported by the strap and two ground stakes. I have never forgotten this image of brutal vandalism. I still don't understand how people are capable of destroying or damaging nature.

Cross(es)
Thank You Marja Hautala

E Sketch
Cesca Murray

One Easter, my Dad painted his egg like a
Cadbury Creme Egg, before rolling it down the hill,
following the British Easter Egg Roll tradition.

My friends Maki, Kaisa, Benjamin, and Patric
from Åbäke told me about a design project
involving eggs that they carried out at a college
in Switzerland. They asked students to construct
a device that would protect an egg from breaking
after being thrown off the roof of the college.
The film they made of the event was hilarious;
the most memorable device was an egg taped
to the center of a frying pan.

Painted Easter egg

Echo
Thank You Tim Metcalf

Background Matching Motorbike
Thank You Sam Graf

Window Reflection
Thank You Simon Jones

Camo Survey
Picture of the Week

No Smoking Sign
Beth (GCSE Student)

Camo Lock 2
Picture of the Week

The Olympic logo was created in 1913 by Pierre de Coubertin. Five interlocking rings—blue, yellow, black, green, and red—represent the five continents.

The Royal Air Force roundel has been associated with pop art of the 1960s, appearing in paintings by Jasper Johns and Peter Blake. It became part of the pop consciousness after the British rock group The Who started to wear RAF roundels as part of their stage apparel at the start of their career. Subsequently, the roundel came to symbolize Mods and has evolved into the icon of cool Britannia.

I proposed a composite of the two icons to form an alternative London 2012 Olympic logo.

I hand drew five hundred circles on A3 sheets. I removed the most accurate one from the stack and framed it, leaving the other 499 sheets as a stack on the floor.

30 mph
Picture of the Week

Hot Pursuit
Picture of the Week

Design Now—London

In 2001 my former studio, Foundation 33, was invited by London's Design Museum to take part in a group show called Design Now—London. Each of the four exhibitors was assigned one of four large glass vitrines on the museum's top floor to display work.

It was the first show instigated by Alice Rawsthorn, the museum's new director, and the first time the museum removed its old, crumbling permanent collection in favor of contemporary work.

At that time Foundation 33 had existed for only one and a bit years, so I called the show a Premature Retrospective 1999–2001 and exhibited all of my Royal College of Art projects, much of the Walker Art Center work, and the Multi Ply furniture made in collaboration with Sam Solhaug.

The exhibit consisted of two components: the glass vitrine in which all printed material was presented horizontally, conceptually echoing the 10.2 Multi Ply Coffee Table's reorientation of plywood; and a platform with undulating heights that elevated the top surfaces of the Multi Ply tables to correspond with the glass vitrine's horizontal surface.

RAC PC
Thank You Simon Jones

Broken Down
Picture of the Week

A-Sign Trestle Table
Picture of the Week

My Flavourite Chicken
Thank You Craig Matchett

Chicken
Thank You Christian Eager

Street Lamp Model Mouth
Thank You Brian Sholis

Slot Sign
Thank You Jake Knight

Chin-Lamped
Thank You Nicole Heinzel

Well Street
Thank You Henrik Kubel

Wellington
Picture of the Week

Stalk
Thank You Paolo Tesei

Pigeon Sandwich
Picture of the Week

THE LINE NAVIGATION TIME TRIAL CHALLENGE

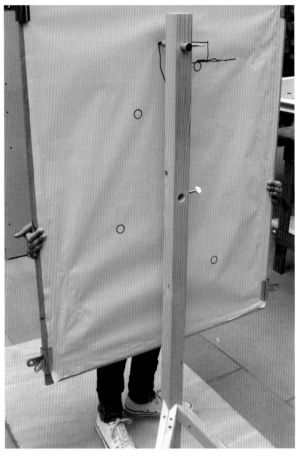

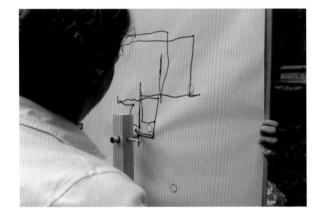

Usually, the easel holds the paper, and the artist holds the pen. Created in 2007 for London's Victoria and Albert Museum's annual V&A Village Fete, the Line Navigation Time Trial Challenge defies this convention.

Two participants stand facing each other. One holds a large sheet of paper and presses it against the nib of a pen that is fixed to the easel. The other gives directions as to how the page needs to be moved in order to draw a line through the five circles pre-printed on the paper. The participant who completes this line in the shortest time possible wins the honor of the top position on the leader board.

Made in collaboration with Mike Jack, Simon Jones, and James Killcross.

Tight Squeeze
Thank You Arran Lidgett

In 2006 I was contacted by a young man called Smitthi Bhiraleus from Thailand, who offered me two thousand pounds to design a logo for his music publishing company. I had never met him and only corresponded via e-mail. I did not expect to receive the payment, but decided to trust him and to see what would happen.

I cut the left top of the capital letter V to form a tick. Very Good ✔

A few weeks later I got paid.
Very good ✔

Thailand & Taiwan

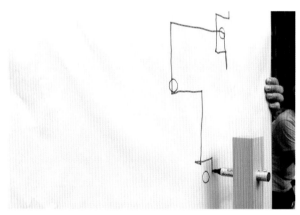

Deviation

Deviation
Picture of the Week

Deviation

Moving
Picture of the Week

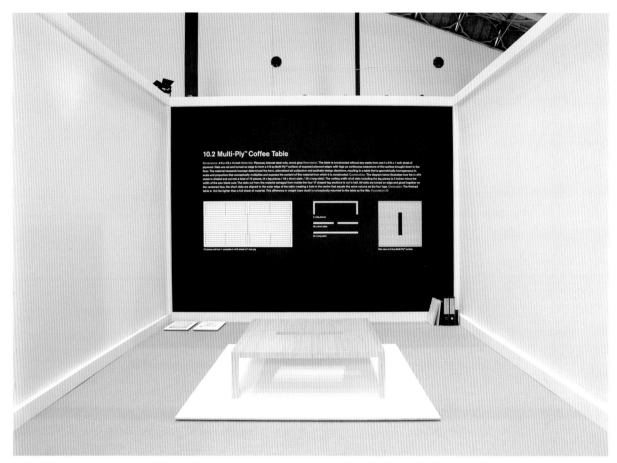

Milan Furniture Fair 2000

Table Arrangement
Picture of the Week

The 10.2 Multi Ply Coffee Table is constructed from a single one-inch-thick 4 x 8 plywood sheet.

The sheet of wood is divided and cut into a total of seventy-two pieces (four leg pieces, forty-eight short slats, twenty long slats).

The cutting width of all slats, including the leg pieces, is two inches minus the width of the saw blade cuts. The slats cut from the salvaged material inside the four U-shaped leg sections are cut in half. All slats are turned on edge and glued together on the veneered face. The short slats are aligned to the outer edge of the table, creating a hole in the center that equals the volume of the four legs. The finished table is 10.2 pounds lighter than the full sheet of wood.

No Sign
Picture of the Week

The World's Largest Signed and Numbered Limited-Edition Artwork took fourteen days to produce. Ten people each signed one hundred thousand postcards; eight people mechanically numbered them with stamping machines; and a project coordinator orchestrated the complex task, making sure that each card was signed, numbered, and packaged in sequence.

A total of 419 A4 boxes each containing 2,400 cards (14 pallets) were signed and numbered.

Each signatory had to sign a card every five seconds, work a ten-hour day, and only take a break of thirty minutes in order to keep on schedule. The artworks were distributed by Boomerang Postcards and were available for free from postcard racks in galleries, coffee bars, restaurants, and movie theaters all over England. We submitted The World's Largest Signed and Numbered Limited-Edition Artwork to the Guinness Book of World Records in January 2003, but it was not accepted because it was an unrecognized category. The project was funded by Channel 4 Television and coincided with the channel's The Art Show, a program about contemporary art and culture.

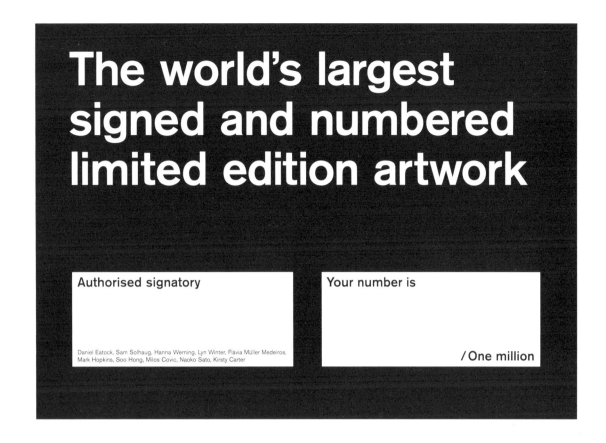

The world's largest signed and numbered limited edition artwork

Authorised signatory

Daniel Eatock, Sam Solhaug, Hanna Werning, Lyn Winter, Flávia Müller Medeiros, Mark Hopkins, Soo Hong, Milos Covic, Naoko Sato, Kirsty Carter

Your number is

/ One million

The number of characters that spell eight trillion and seventeen quintillion match the number of digits when these numbers are written numerically

eighttrillion
8000000000000

seventeenquintillion
17000000000000000000

Supermarket Closed
Picture of the Week

Iron Man
Thank You Michael Place

~~Wheelie~~ Heavy Passenger
Picture of the Week

Signatories:
Daniel Eatock
Sam Solhaug
Hanna Werning
Lyn Winter
Flávia Müller Medeiros
Mark Hopkins
Soo Hong
Milos Covic
Naoko Sato
Kirsty Carter

Helpers:
Sara De Bondt
Billy Boyle
Raymund Brinkmann
Sara Carneholm
Ulrika Flodberg
Charlotte Hopkinson
Mette Iversen
Sarah Labigne
Dawn Parsonage
Kate Pelen
Luna Raphael
Ryan Ras
Sean Rogg
Fran Villani

I would like to give one million people in the world an idea to share.

This idea would be as pretty as a picture.

An idea can be an artwork.

I want one million people to own this artwork.

I want this artwork to be exclusive so you will value it.

I have signed and numbered every artwork.

Does the artist's signature make this artwork exclusive and desirable to you?

You are one of 6,247,210,800 people in the world.

You probably do not own any art.

If one million people own this artwork, there are 6,246,210,800 people that don't.

If you have this artwork you are one in a million.

There is so much art it is impossible to know how to value it.

Do you ever wonder why some things are worth so much and others so little?

I made this card so you might think about how we value things.

I made this card so you would think about how you value yourself.

One Dozen
Thank You Daniella Spinat

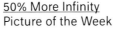

50% More Infinity
Picture of the Week

Self-Protection
Picture of the Week

ABCDEFGHIJKLMNOPQRSTUVWXYZ

Alphabetape is a typeface made from brown packing tape printed onto rolls of transparent tape.

Alphabetape can be used as a text typeface by cutting individual letters from the tape, and as a set of instructions for a display typeface; large letters can be formed with the tape following the shapes of the printed letters.

Hidden Building
Thank You Tom Henni

Notice
Thank You David Parle

Drink Drawing

Draw a straight line, without the aid
of a straight edge, between two points
that are set one meter apart.

Drink one pint of beer, then draw
another straight line between two more
points set one meter apart.

Continue this drawing exercise, drawing
a straight line between two points
set one meter apart after finishing each
pint of beer.

The drawing is complete when the
participant refuses to drink any more.

YES

Nowhere
Thank You Luna Raphael

No No Entry
Picture of the Week

Drunk Pub Table
Picture of the Week

In 2005 the Discovery Channel commissioned me to create a billboard advertising a new genre of history program called Virtual History. Virtual History uses computer-generated imagery technology to recreate moments in history that were never captured on film. The first episode was about a secret plot to kill Hitler during World War II. To advertise the episode I recreated portraits of Winston Churchill and Adolph Hitler in the style of the classic fashion studio shoot as used by Giorgio Armani and Calvin Klein. These portraits looked sexy and contemporary and aimed to shock, confronting the viewer with an image that was difficult to place. The billboard raised questions and started a debate around the ethics of using digital technology to manipulate history.

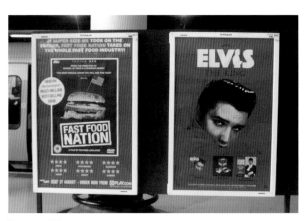

Burger King
Thank You John Anderson

90

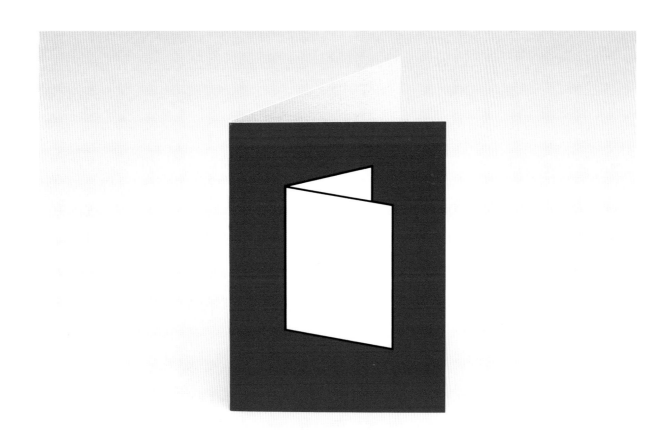

Card Card

London
Thank You Benoit Santiard

Echo
Picture of the Week

Da Boyz
Thank You Robert Leguillon

Aerodynamic Scooter Jacket
Picture of the Week

The Big Brother 3 logo is printed in cyan, magenta, and   (CMYK). None of these pure colors are mixed during the printing process, but they optically mix when the logo is viewed from a distance.

Cyan and   mix to form green.

Magenta and   mix to form red.

Primary Parking
Thank You Mark Owens

CMYK Sheep
Thank You Julia Paass

Primary Hats
Thank You Greg Couple

Coincidence?
Thank You Tunc Topcuoglu

Street Lamp
Picture of the Week

Traffic Light/Cone
Picture of the Week

Complete Roll of Brown Packing Tape Bow

Elephant
Thank You Wayne Daly

Elephant
Thank You Benoit Santiard

The first project I ever had printed was a family Christmas card. I designed it, and my Dad paid to have it printed. It was made in 1996, the same year as the first Government's National Lottery Scratch Card, which I stapled to the front of each card, giving the recipient the chance of winning one hundred thousand pounds.

I am not a gambler but liked the idea of paying one pound to give a friend the chance of winning one hundred thousand. A few people won ten pounds, and Dorothy Whalley mistakenly threw the card away thinking it was junk mail.

Masked Slat Stripes
Picture of the Week

Present
Thank You Manuel Schibli

Peeling
Picture of the Week

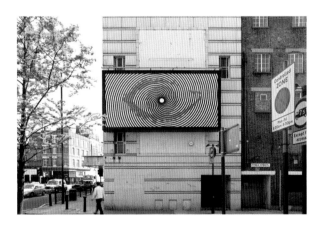

New Skip
Picture of the Week

Approximately half of the <u>Big Brother</u> 7 billboards were accidentally posted upside down. It was an easy mistake, as there was no type or other indicator of the orientation. I like turning things upside down or on their side.

When I was studying at Ravensbourne College I went to visit my friend Ben Parker in his dormitory room at the halls of residence. I threw something in his waste bin, and he removed it and gave it back to me, telling me that he had just emptied it.

I really like obsessions and people trying to be organized and clean, even when it is ridiculous.

Empty Bin
Picture of the Week

I liked my Mum's fruit-stickered clementine so much that she extended this idea to make a fruit bowl covered with fruit stickers. She intended to give it to me as a present, but I hated the square bowl she used. I accepted the idea as a present instead and made my own version on a round bowl.

There is a red, a white, and a blue van on this spread to match the image below.

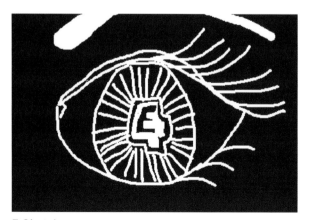

E Sketch
Ceri-Anne Thomas

USAutomobiles
Thank You Derek Maxwell

Celebrity <u>Big Brother</u> logo

<u>Transit Fan</u>
Thank You Mark Hopkins

<u>Car a Van (Car Caravan Van)</u>
Picture of the Week

<u>Neat Fly Tipping</u>
Picture of the Week

I arranged a complete set of Letraset Tria Pantone markers in the order of the color spectrum and left them for one month, resting on their nibs, on a stack of five hundred SRA1 sheets of 70 gsm uncoated white paper.

The numbering and value of each sheet corresponds to its position within the stack. The final sheet the ink reached (out of the stack of five hundred) was numbered 1/73 and valued at one pound; the one above it was numbered 2/73 and valued at two pounds; and so on. The top sheet (the sheet the pens rested on directly) was numbered 73/73 and valued at seventy-three pounds.

Untitled
Don Matheson and Simon Jones

Black and Gold Sign / Black and Gold Bin

Black Chair and Bin / Gold Foam and Graffiti
Picture of the Week

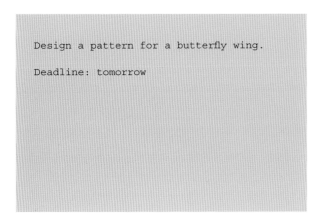

```
Design a pattern for a butterfly wing.

Deadline: tomorrow
```

Rubbish Flower
Picture of the Week

Imagine an artwork purposely structured to produce random prints with no control over the way they look. Imagine the audience is expected to buy these random prints without knowing what they look like.

The audience had to choose a print edition number between 1 and 500 based on an abstract judgement of how many sheets would ultimately be included within the edition, and what they could afford to pay. The sheet number correspond to the amount the audience would pay for the print, resulting in prints sold from £1 to a potential £500.

It was a game, and the audience played. All prints was sold. The ink reached sheet 73. The rest of the white stack was not marked. If you had chosen number 100, you would have lost your betting and print. On the other hand, numbers 1 to 73 were in for the game. They were going like hot cakes! The audience sometimes looked excited without knowing why, and bought the work, to risk, to be surprised, to participate.

However, the most interesting point was not the surprise later at home when they opened the tube in which the paid print was packaged and finally saw what they had bought at the gallery. What really mattered was the collective excitement in the gallery space and the decision to believe in something they couldn't see. Almost like a transcendental experience. The money was just part of it.

FMM

Print 12 of 73

Two Car Family
Thank You Nick Hand

108

Big Brother 4 logo

Urban 4x4 School Run
Picture of the Week

4x4x4x4
Thank You Nigel Ball

Family
Picture of the Week

<u>Stone Sculpture</u>
Urquhart Castle, Loch Ness, Inverness, Scotland

<u>Chalk Drawing</u>
White Horse, Uffington, Oxfordshire, England

Big Brother 4 logo billboard

The Guardian newspaper referred to the Big Brother landmarks, commissioned by Channel 4 in 2003 to promote series four, as "brandalism."

I liked that a new word had to be invented to describe what was made.

The Big Brother stone sculpture, constructed near Loch Ness with permission by Historic Scotland, took a crew of ten people about ten hours to complete. Approximately fifteen tons of limestone from a local quarry were delivered to the site, and the eye was visible for forty-eight hours before it was removed by the crew.

The Big Brother chalk eye was painted with permission by the National Trust above the mysterious White Horse, which was carved into the chalk hillside above the village of Uffington in Oxfordshire over three thousand years ago. The eye was made using an environmentally friendly chalk-based paint and took eight hours to finish. It was later removed using high-power water jets.

Reflection
Picture of the Week

Outcast
Picture of the Week

111

Crop Circle
Private field, Oxfordshire, England

Sand Drawing
Carmarthenshire, Wales

The <u>Big Brother</u> crop circle was made in a rapeseed field, the most mature crop at this time of year. The one-hundred-meter-wide crop circle took six people a total of seven hours to construct.

The <u>Big Brother</u> sand drawing was sixty-five meters wide and took a crew of six people over six hours to construct. The window between high and low tide left only eight hours to build and photograph the drawing. The darker patterns in the wet sand were created by removing dry areas of sand.

<u>E Sketch</u>
Lucy Gale

<u>Big Brother</u> 5 logo

<u>Puncture Repair Truck</u>
Picture of the Week

<u>Puffer Fish (deflated)</u>
Picture of the Week

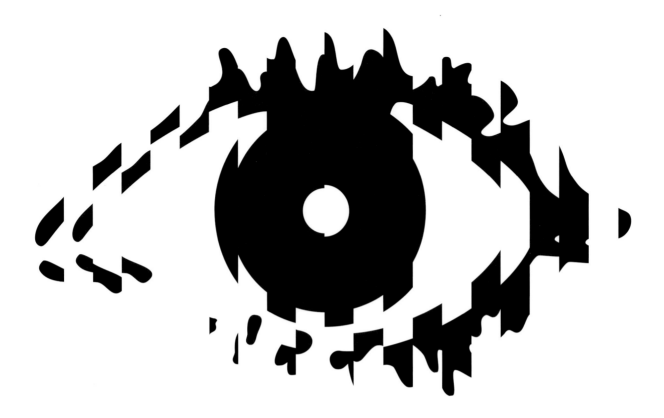

Big Brother 6 logo

One year later Channel 4 wanted to create something equally spectacular as a follow-up to the large-scale landmark eye logos. A few weeks earlier, IKEA had opened a store in Edmonton and offered a sofa for five pounds. Many more people than expected turned up to buy a sofa; IKEA inevitably sold out; and riots started in the parking lot, with customers fighting over sofas.

Brett Foraker, the creative director at Channel 4, used this as his inspiration. "Let's create something fans will fight over!" he declared.

I art-directed the construction of my eye logo from one thousand and twenty boxes, six hundred of which contained television sets. Big Brother fans were informed and invited to grab a box. The semi-organized chaos was filmed for an on-air trailer that showed the eye being swamped and broken apart by fans.

114

Support
Thank You Corey Holms

Red Man, Do Not Cross
Picture of the Week

Tree Construction
Picture of the Week

Big Brother 7 logo

Daily Star logo rumor

A week before the new <u>Big Brother</u> 7 identity went public, the <u>Daily Star</u> newspaper ran a special feature on it, and Lindsay Nuttall from Channel 4 asked me to write a few words about the design. I initially listed statements that were obvious from looking at the logo—"The yellow and black are like the sting of a bee. The spiral is like the eye of a hurricane." When I realized how descriptive and redundant my text was, I replaced it with the following:

"This year's logo has been designed to be hypnotic and conceals a subliminal secret for viewers to discover. To view the hidden secret, stare at the center of the eye and rotate it slowly and smoothly for at least twenty seconds— even longer, to enhance the effect—and then look at a light-colored surface or a white piece of paper. A secret message will be produced on the retina. If the direction of rotation is reversed, the message will also be reversed. If you are not able to see the secret message, try to defocus your eyes and rotate the eye even slower. Once you have discovered the hidden secret, please do not tell others— allow them to discover it for themselves."

96-sheet billboard

<u>Hazard Light</u>
Thank You Simon Jones

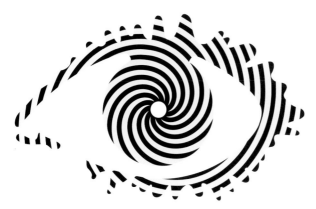
<u>Big Brother</u> 7 press logo

<u>Floor Markings</u>
Picture of the Week

<u>Digital Malfunction</u>
Thank You Simon Jones

<u>Train Truck</u>
Picture of the Week

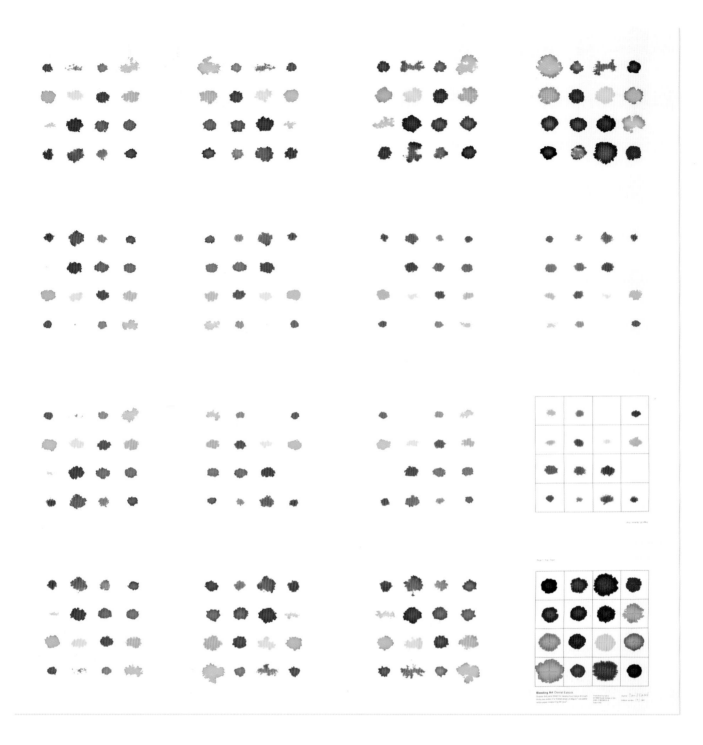

While at the Royal College of Art, I became interested in setting up systems that create work themselves. I constructed a wooden support that held sixteen felt-tip pens in a grid, and then left it with the pens uncapped to bleed for twenty-four hours through thirty-two sides of a folded sheet of 80 gsm uncoated white paper measuring 841 millimeters square.

The unfolded sheet displays each pen's layered bleed marks. The slipcase diagrams map the ink's path through the sheets and the orientation of each folded page.

Made in an edition of three hundred copies.

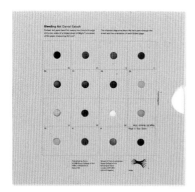

Big Brother 8 logo

Sky Windows
Thank You Ryan Thacker

Sky Blue
Picture of the Week

Shark
Picture of the Week

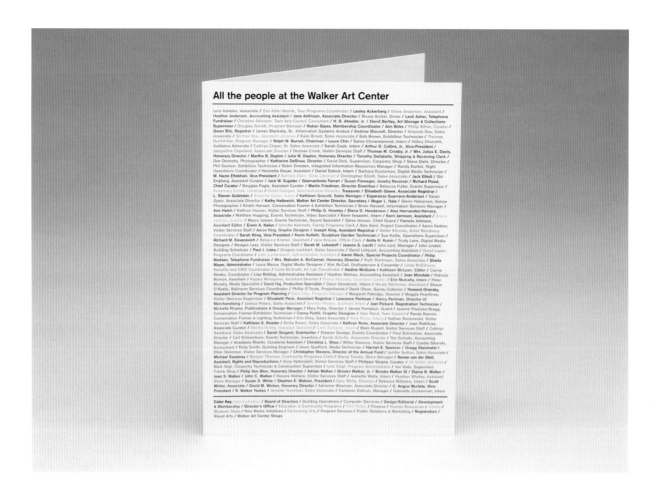

All the people at the Walker Art Center

Lora Aadalen, Associate / Zoe Adler-Resnik, Tour Programs Coordinator / Lesley Ackerberg / Diane Anderson, Assistant / Heather Anderson, Accounting Assistant / Jane Anfinson, Associate Director / Bruce Archer, Driver / Lesli Asher, Telephone Fundraiser / Christine Atkinson, Teen Arts Council Consultant / H. B. Atwater, Jr. / David Bartley, Art Storage & Collections Supervisor / Douglas Benidt, Program Manager / Robyn Bipes, Membership Coordinator / Ann Birks / Philip Bither, Curator / Gwen Bitz, Registrar / James Blackaby, Sr., Information Systems Analyst / Andrew Blauvelt, Director / Amanda Bloe, Sales Associate / Michele Boe, Assistant Librarian / Kaile Brood, Sales Associate / Bob Brown, Exhibition Technician / Therese Buchmiller, Program Manager / Ralph W. Burnet, Chairman / Laura Chin / Sylvia Chivaratanond, Intern / Hillary Churchill, Audience Advocate / Cathryn Cloper, Sr. Sales Associate / Sarah Cook, Intern / Arthur D. Collins, Jr., Vice-President / Jacqueline Copeland, Associate Director / Desiree Cronk, Visitor Services Staff / Thomas M. Crosby, Jr. / Mrs. Julius E. Davis, Honorary Director / Martha B. Dayton / Julia W. Dayton, Honorary Director / Timothy Dellabella, Shipping & Receiving Clerk / Dan Dennehy, Photographer / Katharine DeShaw, Director / David Dick, Supervisor, Carpentry Shop / Steve Dietz, Director / Phil Docken, Exhibition Technician / Robin Dowden, Integrated Information Resources Manager / Randy Durbin, Night Operations Coordinator / Henrietta Dwyer, Assistant / Daniel Eatock, Intern / Barbara Economon, Digital Media Technician / M. Nazie Eftekhari, Vice-President / Barbara Elam, Slide Librarian / Christopher Elliott, Sales Associate / Jack Elliott / Siri Engberg, Assistant Curator / Jack W. Eugster / Giannantonio Ferrari / Susan Fieweger, Jewelry Receiver / Richard Flood, Chief Curator / Douglas Fogle, Assistant Curator / Martin Friedman, Director Emeritus / Rebecca Fuller, Events Supervisor / Rosemary Furtak, Librarian / David Galligan, Administrative Director, Treasurer / Elisabeth Glawe, Associate Registrar / L. Steven Goldstein / Amanda Green, Intern / Kathleen Grocott, Sales Manager / Esperanza Guerrero-Anderson / Karen Gysin, Associate Director / Kathy Halbreich, Walker Art Center Director, Secretary / Roger L. Hale / Glenn Halvorson, Senior Photographer / Kirstin Hanson, Conservation Framer & Exhibition Technician / Brian Hassett, Information Services Manager / Ann Hatch / Kathryn Hauser, Visitor Services Staff / Philip G. Heasley / Elena D. Henderson / Alex Hernandez-Herrera, Associate / Matthew Hopping, Events Technician, Video Specialist / Kemi Ilesanmi, Intern / Kerri Jamison, Assistant / Bruce Jenkins, Curator / Maury Jensen, Events Technician, Sound Specialist / Steve Jensen, Chief Guard / Pamela Johnson, Assistant Editor / Erwin A. Kelen / Jennifer Kennedy, Family Programs Clerk / Alex Kent, Project Coordinator / Aaron Kesher, Visitor Services Staff / Aaron King, Graphic Designer / Joseph King, Assistant Registrar / Walter Kitundu, Artist Residency Coordinator / Sarah Kling, Vice-President / Kevin Kolleth, Sculpture Garden Technician / Sue Kotila, Operations Supervisor / Richard M. Kovacevich / Rebecca Kramer, Assistant / Jace Krause, Office Clerk / Anita H. Kunin / Trudy Lane, Digital Media Designer / Meagan Lass, Visitor Services Staff / Sarah M. Lebedoff / Jeanne S. Levitt / John Lied, Manager / John Lindell, Building Scheduler / Paul J. Liska / Gregory Lockhart, Sales Associate / David Lofquist, Accounting Assistant / David Logan, Programs Coordinator / Julie Luckenbach, Administrative Assistant / Aaron Mack, Special Projects Coordinator / Philip Madsen, Telephone Fundraiser / Mrs. Malcolm A. McCannel, Honorary Director / Ruth Martinsen, Sales Associate / Sheila Mayer, Administrator / Louis Mazza, Digital Media Designer / Kirk McCall, Draftsperson & Carpenter / Linda McElmurry, Benefits and HRIS Coordinator / Curla McGrath, Art Lab Coordinator / Nadine McGuire / Kathleen McLean, Editor / Camie Meaks, Coordinator / Lisa Middag, Administrative Assistant / Heather Molnau, Accounting Assistant / Joan Mondale / Patricia Monick, Assistant / Kiyoko Motoyama, Assistant Director / Sheryl Mousley, Assistant Curator / Erin Mulcahy, Intern / Peter Murphy, Media Specialist / David Naj, Production Specialist / Dawn Newstrom, Intern / Nicole Nitchman, Assistant / Shaun O'Keefe, Mailroom Services Coordinator / Phillip O'Toole, Projectionist / David Olson, Survey Collector / Howard Oransky, Assistant Director for Program Planning / Dean Otto, Program Manager / Margaret Patridge, Director / Maggie Pearthree, Visitor Services Supervisor / Elizabeth Peck, Assistant Registrar / Lawrence Perlman / Nancy Perlman, Director of Merchandising / Joshua Peters, Sales Associate / Jennifer Phelps, Archives Intern / Joel Pickard, Registration Technician / Michelle Piranio, Publications & Design Manager / Mary Polta, Director / James Pomplun, Guard / Jeanne Prezioso-Bragg, Conservation Framer/Exhibition Technician / Conny Purtill, Graphic Designer / Alex Rand, Teen Council / Randy Reeves, Conservation Framer & Lighting Technician / Erin Riley, Sales Associate / Ana Rizzo, Intern / Nathan Rockswold, Visitor Services Staff / Kathleen S. Roeder / Rollie Rosen, Sales Associate / Kathryn Ross, Associate Director / Joan Rothfuss, Associate Curator / Martha Ruddy, Assistant Archivist / Cami Rutisand, Intern / Mark Rupert, Visitor Services Staff / Cathryn Sandlund, Sales Associate / Sarah Sargent, Grantwriter / Eleanor Savage, Events Coordinator / Paul Schmelzer, Associate Director / Carl Schoenborn, Events Technician, Inventory / Sarah Schultz, Associate Director / Tim Schultz, Accounting Manager / Anastasia Shartin, Curatorial Assistant / Christina L. Shea / Writer Siasoco, Visitor Services Staff / Cyndie Sikorski, Accountant / Kelsy Smith, Building Engineer / Jason Spafford, Media Technician / Harriet S. Spencer / Gregg Steinhafel / Ellen Steinman, Visitor Services Manager / Christopher Stevens, Director of the Annual Fund / Jenifer Sutton, Sales Associate / Michael Sweeney / Morgan Thorson, Community Programs Clerk / Sheryl Tuorila, Store Manager / Renee van der Stelt, Assistant, Rights and Reproductions / Anne Vaflendahl, Visitor Services Staff / Philippe Vergne, Curator / Jill Vetter, Archivist / Mark Vogt, Carpentry Technician & Construction Supervisor / Julie Voigt, Program Administrator / Jon Vails, Supervisor, Frame Shop / Philip Von Blon, Honorary Director / Adrian Walker / Brooks Walker, Jr. / Brooks Walker III / Elaine B. Walker / Jean S. Walker / John C. Walker / Roxane Wallace, Visitor Services Staff / Jeanette Wells, Intern / Heather Whaley, Assistant Store Manager / Susan S. White / Stephen E. Watson, President / Gary White, Director / Rebecca Williams, Intern / Scott Winter, Associate / David M. Winton, Honorary Director / Adrienne Wiseman, Associate Director / C. Angus Wurtele, Vice-President / R. Walker Yeates / Jennifer Yurchisin, Sales Associate / Cameron Zebrun, Manager / Gabrielle Zuckerman, Intern

Color Key: Administration / Board of Directors / Building Operations / Computer Services / Design/Editorial / Development & Membership / Director's Office / Education & Community Programs / Film Video / Finance / Human Resources / Library / Museum Shop / New Media Initiatives / Performing Arts / Program Services / Public Relations & Marketing / Registration / Visual Arts / Walker Art Center Shops

Rubber Stamp

120

My first design project as an intern for the Walker Art Center was the museum's 1998 Christmas card. I compiled a list of every person who worked at the Walker, arranged it in alphabetical order, and color-coordinated the names based on each person's department.

During my time at the Walker Art Center I designed all single-color print projects in black. Just before the design went to print, I would ask Michele Piranio, the studio manager, to choose a color. I would then replace the black with the chosen color in the Quark document and have a color design with one click. Michele became a part of my objective design process. She negated the need for me to make a subjective decision and became another standard, helping me rationalize as many decisions as possible within the design process.

I sometimes wish there was a less subjective way of selecting color for single-color print jobs. The last time I went to the Walker Art Center's design department, the designers showed me a big envelope full of old Pantone chips—they joked that they select color by a lucky dip.

Thief
Thank You Alfred Strik Swages

E Sketch
Andrew McCormack

Matching Car Doors
Picture of the Week

Green Car Green Clamp

Drainpipe Tree
Picture of the Week

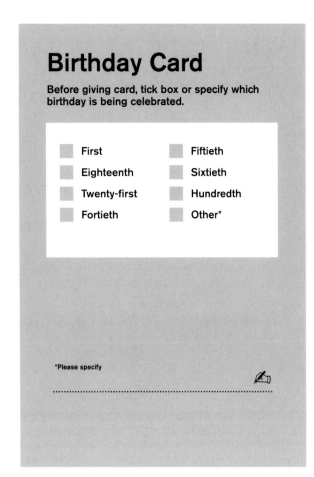

Birthday Card

Before giving card, tick box or specify which birthday is being celebrated.

- First
- Eighteenth
- Twenty-first
- Fortieth
- Fiftieth
- Sixtieth
- Hundredth
- Other*

*Please specify

....

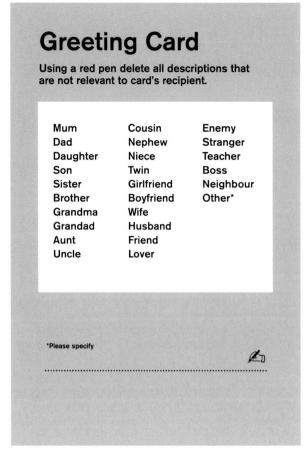

Greeting Card

Using a red pen delete all descriptions that are not relevant to card's recipient.

Mum	Cousin	Enemy
Dad	Nephew	Stranger
Daughter	Niece	Teacher
Son	Twin	Boss
Sister	Girlfriend	Neighbour
Brother	Boyfriend	Other*
Grandma	Wife	
Grandad	Husband	
Aunt	Friend	
Uncle	Lover	

*Please specify

....

While I attended the Royal College of Art, the chain store Marks & Spencer invited students to propose ideas for products. I suggested a set of Utilitarian Greeting Cards that rely on the sender to appropriate them for the recipient.

Marks & Spencer hated the cards, but I loved them and printed five hundred of each design, in the hope of selling the cards to earn some pocket money. Nobody bought any. Three years later, when I returned to London after working at the Walker Art Center, I started to sell the cards at the Institute of Contemporary Arts in London, and a few other shops. So far I have reprinted them seventeen times—each time I change the color printed on the inside.

Like most people, I collect stuff—letters, postcards, photographs, notes—anything that is special to me and that I do not want to dispose of. Naturally, this adds clutter to my daily life.

Timecapstool is a box with a narrow slot on the top. It is designed to hold ephemera, which can easily be inserted through the slot, and at the same time function as a stool, a step, or a side table.

Once something has been posted into the slot, there is no easy means to retrieve it: the stool is sealed on all sides. Over time, the ephemera inside becomes more important than the stool. At this point the Timecapstool can be smashed open like a piggy bank.

The stool is not intended to be opened for five years. The longer it is used, the more valuable and interesting the contents will be when eventually retrieved by the owner.

Left-out Bricks
Picture of the Week

Away
Picture of the Week

UTILITARIAN (DELETE AS NECESSARY) ADVERTISEMENT/ANNOUNCEMENT/BULLETIN/DECLARATION/PROCLAMATION

THIS POSTER PROVIDES A FRAME & STRUCTURE FOR THE INFORMATION & DETAILS FOR ANY EVENT/HAPPENING
COMPLETE THE EIGHT SECTIONS BELOW USING ANY METHOD OR MEDIUM
CONCEPT & DESIGN COPYRIGHT DANIEL EATOCK 1998 SAY YES TO FUN & FUNCTION & NO TO SEDUCTIVE IMAGERY & COLOUR!

TITLE

DESCRIPTION OF EVENT/HAPPENING   DATE   TIME

DIAGRAM/DOODLE/DRAWING/IMAGE/PAINTING/PHOTOGRAPH/SCRIBBLE/ETCETERA

LOCATION/ADDRESS   DIRECTIONS/MAP

FURTHER INFORMATION

IF YOU WOULD LIKE COPIES OF THE UTILITARIAN POSTER FOR ANY FORTHCOMING EVENT/HAPPENING CONTACT:
DANIEL EATOCK/SCHOOL OF COMMUNICATION DESIGN/ROYAL COLLEGE OF ART/KENSINGTON GORE/LONDON/SW7 2EU/UNITED KINGDOM
TELEPHONE + 44 171 590 4444 EXTENSION 4311/FACSIMILE + 44 171 590 4300

POSTER COMPLETED BY

Wiped Clean
Thank You Timothy Evans

A generic template silk-screened on newsprint methodically guides users through the steps of creating their own advertisements. The template includes blanks in which to insert relevant information such as titles of events, images, persons to contact, and so on. The work is wholly dependent on viewer response—its absence denies the piece its essential content.

Say "yes" to fun and function and "no" to seductive imagery and color!

Late Card

Write an excuse or apology in no more than fifty words to explain why this card is late.

Sign and date

....

Occasion Card

Before giving card, tick the box relevant to the occasion being celebrated.

Birthday	New Year
Valentine	Anniversary
Mother's Day	Good luck
Easter	Congratulations
Father's Day	Well done
Christmas	Other*

*Please specify

....

Camera Strap
Sam Stephens

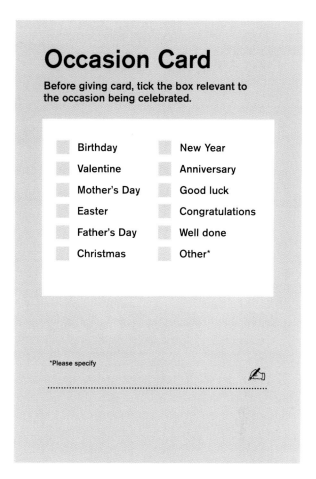

Hot Pursuit
Picture of the Week

Postcard
Picture of the Week

In 2005 I designed a catalog in collaboration with artists Oliver Payne and Nick Relph to coincide with their show at the Serpentine Gallery in London.

Camo Charlotte

I find it hard to collaborate, but I am always eager to try. I don't like designers who never compromise—I like getting suggestions from others. Maki, a designer from Åbäke, told me the story of a difficult client who was very controlling of a project to design a poster: he wanted the title to be in bold, the e-mail address to be red, all the names to be bigger, and so on. I have never seen the finished poster, but I like the idea of it: an awkward hybrid of considered design with input and art direction from the client.

Working with Oliver and Nick was not exactly like that, but they did have some very specific ideas of what the exhibition catalog should look like. Being a fan of their films, I was open to forming the book as a collaboration, to result in something special that captured the essence and spontaneity of their practice.

The catalog's many parts and details—London Transport fabric cover, a cell phone ringtone sound-chip, reproductions of rubber stamps, photographs, handwritten notes, a flip-book smiley face, German translations, essays, an interview, a selection of invited submissions, and input from the copublishers, Kunsthalle Zürich—combined with a very tight deadline and a tight budget, made it the most complex book I have ever designed, but now that it is completed, it looks like the simplest one.

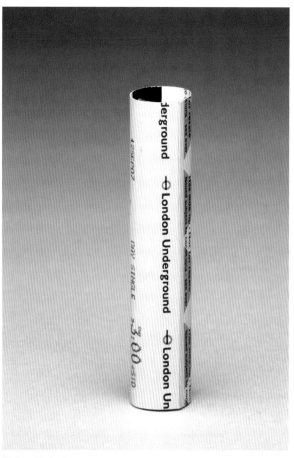

Tube Ticket

Tricycle Parking
Thank You Nicolas and Nadia

Rubbish Pram Parking
Picture of the Week

Tie-Dye

Dan Flavin at Bank
Picture of the Week

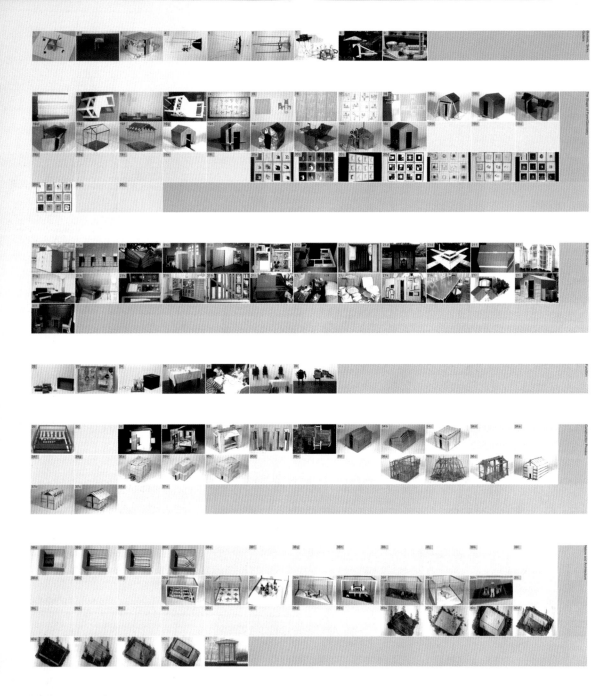

Custom Built: A Twenty-Year Survey of Work by Allan Wexler

Tape Race

I have been fascinated with all kinds of tape and have acquired a large collection, including masking tape, Sellotape, duct tape, electrical tape, magic tape, packaging tape, and double-sided tape. Each time I travel, I bring home a new tape specimen—high-tech, ultra-sticky, reflective, heat-resistant, tear-resistant, or multicolored. I have made a number of works that explore the properties of my tape collection: I have recoiled a complete role of red tape around my steel table leg. I have unraveled a complete roll of brown packaging tape in a pile on the floor and stuck it on a gallery wall. I have unraveled a complete roll of tear-resistant tape and attached the two ends between two fixed points. I have coiled a complete roll of red duct tape around the two walls, ceiling, and floor of a gallery.

For a show at M+R Gallery, called The Free Library, I stuck my collection of tape rolls on a steel beam and left them to slowly unwind down to the floor. The different combinations of weight and adhesiveness resulted in an unpredictable race. The brown tape was the winner; the masking tape came in second; and the red tape came in third.

I would like to stick a full role of masking tape in one long straight line and then keep adding new rolls below until the length of the unraveled roles is matched by the multiple line widths, forming one enormous masking tape square.

Small Medium Large
Picture of the Week

Creepy Crawly
Picture of the Week

People usually remove the price labels from an object before giving it away as a present.

Using Price Label Wrapping Paper, a present can be completely covered in price labels, calling into question the consumerist obsession with a gift's monetary value and the act of giving.

Camera Strap
James Greenfield

Tinted Widow
Thank You Sam Mallett

Cutout Tree
Thank You Timothy Evans

Elephant Foot
Picture of the Week

Rip Off
Thank You Christian

Sellotape Corner Confetti
Picture of the Week

Our friends Martin and Lou invited Flávia and me to accompany them to a dog show at Earls Court. They love dogs. I hate dogs. Flávia loves dogs. I love new things. So we went. I was interested in the similarities between the dogs' hair and their owners' hair.

Baby Guard Dog
Thank You Matus Kissa

Romanian Canine Ref. GMB 5
Thank You Tim Geldmacher

Matching Dogs
Picture of the Week

Fly Wheel
Picture of the Week

Car Alarm Dance 1

I spent February and March 2007 living and working in Vilnius, the capital of Lithuania. During my stay I noticed that car alarms were constantly interrupting the peace. The alarms were so sensitive that even a whisper would set them off.

I invented a theory that some German car alarm manufacturer had made a bad batch of alarms and, rather than throwing them away, exported them to Lithuania and sold them cheap. Due to their economic circumstances, Lithuanians are desperate for a bargain and also eager to prove they have a car that is worth stealing.

Car Alarm Dance 2

The car alarm was like the Lacoste crocodile: a status symbol worn proudly, bleeping when switched on and off and reminding everyone within a siren's distance that THIS CAR IS WORTH STEALING!

One day, out of sheer frustration, I left my desk, found the car whose alarm had been interrupting my peace every five minutes, and waited patiently for the siren to switch on. When the siren sounded, I started dancing like a madman. I proceeded to make videos of several of my car alarm dances, never touching the car, only dancing to the sound pollutants.

Car Alarm Dance 3

I was recently contacted by Sascha Lee from Saatchi & Saatchi, a large advertising agency, who asked if they could use the car alarm dance movies in a T-Mobile advertisement for five hundred pounds. I thought my dancing was pretty good and, disappointed by the amount offered, declined his invitation. He called back a few days later and offered twice as much. I declined again, saying I would not sell for less than £10,000. Everything went quiet, and I thought I had blown it. Then I got an e-mail and we settled for £10,000.

I was very happy to sell the videos for use in a commercial context. This is my dream: to make work independently from commissions and then sell the rights to art directors or advertisers.

Car Alarm Dance 4

In the late 1980s and early 1990s, the underground rave scene reached a peak in Great Britain. As the last excesses of an increasingly totalitarian Thatcherite government intensified, the Criminal Justice Act was passed in Parliament. This prohibited, as I remember it, 'gatherings' of more than four individuals in venues where repetitive beats could be heard.

To an increasingly pilled-up and blissed-out group of hardcore ravers, this was seen, quite rightly, as a fundamental invasion of human rights. There were many acts of defiance, including — when police raided warehouse parties — evicted ravers dancing to the 'repetitive beats' of squad car and riot van sirens pulled up outside the venue.

To this day, my friend Will and I — despite the fact that we are now in our mid-thirties and attempting to hold down senior management positions — will wave our hands in the air like idiots if we hear police sirens.

Those were the days.

(Bill Griffin, former head of marketing at Channel 4)

Trick Jump Chair
Picture of the Week

Carnoe
Picture of the Week

Symmetry
Thank You Eric Wrenn

Reflection
Thank You Kevin Scully

New Friends
Thank You Tomohide Mizuuchi

V Double W
Thank You Tim Metcalf

A Pear

Umbrella Handle and Drain Outlet
Picture of the Week

Bottoms Up
Thank You Alfred Strik Swages

Swan Neck and Monkey Tail (with banana)
Picture of the Week

Electric Chair, 1967
Lambeth Palace Road

The Million Edition Rubber Stamp was originally
created in 1994 to stamp the backs of handmade
greeting cards I was making and selling in small
gift shops and boutiques. It was an ironic joke, as
I considered one million of anything too large a
quantity to be considered limited.

I have always been interested in the idea of limited
editions—that by limiting the number of something
the perceived value is increased due to exclusivity.
I also have an interest in mass production and
massive quantities of identical objects.

Sand Sofa
Thank You Gavin Day

Irish Chairs
Thank You Adam Hayes

Luxury Bus Stop
Thank You Bill Hunt

138

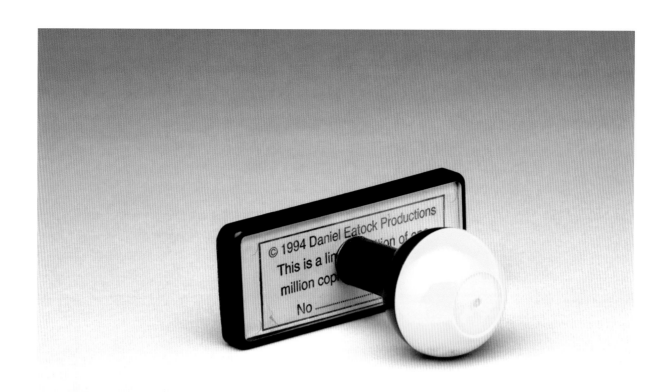

Rubbish Chair
Picture of the Week

Hot Medium Cold
Thank You Steve Lea

Stand
Picture of the Week

Hi Daniel,

Hope all's well. Just wondered if you fancied
having a crack at Letterform this month? It's
the piece where we ask you to pick one of your
favorite characters and write a short piece
about it. We then show the letter as large as
possible on the page opposite the text.

What I'd need from you is anything up to three
hundred words, plus an EPS of the character
in question and a screen-res PDF for reference.
I'd need it by Monday, 25 June. Let me know
what you think...

BW

Caroline Roberts
Editor, Grafik Magazine

Hello Caroline,

Choosing a single character from a single
typeface? That's a pretty tough task. My
type-choosing ability is limited to well-known
standards, nothing that attracts too much
attention, and typefaces that feel archetypal.

Your e-mail invitation was typed in Monaco,
and I always thought this font's slashed 0 was
nice. It reminds me of the "No" symbol often
used for "No Smoking" signs.

Best,

Dan

Slashed Zero
wikipedia.org/wiki/Slashed_zero

The slashed zero looks just like a regular letter
O or number 0 (zero), but it has a slash through it.
Unlike the Scandinavian vowel Ø and the empty set
symbol, the slash often touches the walls of the
surrounding O shape but does not extend past them
on the outside. It is used as the glyph for the
number 0 on character displays in mainframe and
some personal computers to distinguish the letter
O from the number 0.

The slashed zero, looking identical to the letter
O other than the slash, is used in many ASCII graphic
sets descended from the default typewheel on the
Model 33 Teletype. Interestingly, the slashed zero
long predates computers, and has been known to have
been used in the twelfth and thirteenth centuries.

The slashed zero symbol is widely used in written
Amateur radio callsigns, New Zealand alphanumeric
car number plates, codes for video-games, software
product keys, and any other instance when clarity
is necessary.

No Smoking Sign
Ben Harris

In 2005 I was involved in a project that was trying to make Samsung into a contemporary brand.

I proposed that the quickest and most intelligent way forward was to remove the Samsung logo (badge) from all its products, since Samsung is a company whose main concern is technology, not brands. Samsung would still brand its advertising, retail outlets, and packaging, but all its goods would be de-badged. Through negation of the logo, the Samsung brand becomes sophisticated and understated, like a clothing brand whose designer chooses to remove the "1990s designer" logo labels and subtly suggests the brand through quality and use of materials.

What does this say? Multinational corporations need to improve their brands not through clever use of logos, but by making better products. Examples of large companies that defined their brand through quality and function include MUJI and Marks & Spencer: both sell unbranded goods, and both have a strong brand identity through the quality and simplicity of their products.

Could Samsung make Sony and other market leaders look dated and old-fashioned in the same way that clothing brands with logos and motifs on the pockets look outdated today?

Without a logo, Samsung would become the only nonbranded appliance manufacturer. That's a refreshing thought—a home without logos.

When I was about ten or eleven, my Dad bought a brand-new Volkswagen Golf GTI. On the day he picked it up, he drove the car back home, carefully removed all the badges from the trunk of the car, filled the holes, masked the area, and resprayed the panel. Nobody knew what model he drove. I think Mercedes now charges customers extra for doing exactly the same thing.

An additional last thought e-mailed from my Dad: "On your subject of branding, Armani does an interesting job on his jeans collection: on his cheap jeans he plasters his logo all over; on his middle range it's more discreet; and on his top range there's nothing visible on the outside."

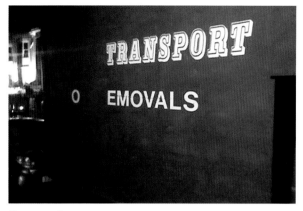
Removed
Thank You Oliver Hydes

Blue Sign Blue Lorry
Thank You David Darnes

A Sign
Picture of the Week

Illuminated Lucozade and Leaves
Picture of the Week

See-Through

Blank Reaction

1. Record an audience listening to
a blank cassette tape on full volume.
End the recording when a member of
the audience reacts.

2. Record a new audience listening
to the recording of the first audience
listening and reacting to the blank
cassette tape. End the recording
when a member of the audience reacts.

3. Repeat step two until the blank
cassette tape consists only of reactions
to a blank cassette tape.

New audiences may react before or
after previous audiences.

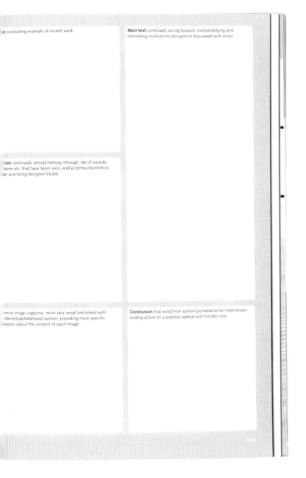

Mosquitos are repelled by the audio frequency twenty kilohertz, which is not discernable by the human ear. I would like to record three minutes of a twenty kilohertz tone on a CD, and release and promote it during summertime as an "Audio Mosquito Repellent."

If it is successful, it may get radio airplay and even enter the music charts as a silent hit.

LEA
Picture of the Week

Five Legs
Picture of the Week

143

Prit Stick Stuck on Ceiling

Solo show at Kemistry Gallery December 2007
Installation shot

Complete role of red duct tape coiled around
gallery walls, floor and ceiling

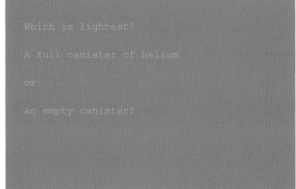

Logo for Channel 4's morning news and entertainment program

I would like to make the smallest ton.

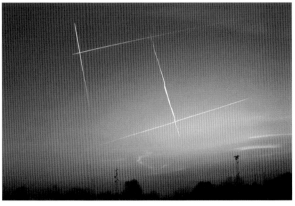

Jet Square
Thank You James Hope-Falkner

Blueloon
Picture of the Week

Plane Train
Picture of the Week

Extended Arm
Thank You Colm Roche

Extended Line

Victorialign
Thank You Joshua Williams

Align

Jump
Thank You So Hashizume

Jumper
Picture of the Week

Track Lighting
Picture of the Week

DIY Pen Extension Challenge: Name-Writing Stretch was invented in 2003 for the Victoria and Albert Museum's V&A Village Fete.

"Design and construct a pen extension with which to write your given name or initials (if your name is longer than ten letters) while standing as far away from a vertical sheet of A1 paper as possible.

You will be measured from any point on the paper to the closest point on the ground that you touch while drawing.

Good luck constructing your distance-defying lettering lance!"

Made in collaboration with Louis Bonnet.

Prosthetic Limb
Thank You Jon Lane-Smith

Branch
Picture of the Week

Beijing Road Sweeper
Picture of the Week

State of Play

Maurizio Cattelan
Martin Creed
Tony Feher
Christian Jankowski
Gabriel Kuri
Bjørn Melhus
Aleksandra Mir
Tim Noble and Sue Webster
Pipilotti Rist
David Shrigley
Andreas Slominski
Sarah Sze

The Serpentine Gallery's 2004 State of Play exhibition catalog was designed to be available for people to buy on the night of the private opening. To make this possible, the catalog was printed in two parts:

Part one was a book designed and printed in advance of the show, featuring reproductions of the twelve artists' past works. Part two was a set of twelve postcards documenting the works in situ in the Serpentine Gallery, printed the night before the private opening and inserted within the book.

The catalog and postcards are held together with a selection of colored elastic bands that the printed cover playfully camouflages.

Color-Coded Grit Boxes
Thank You Gavin Day

Flávia's Grandma, pink camo

Flávia's Mum and cousin, red and orange camo

Flávia, Dan, Val, Simon, and stranger

We were all wearing green on the same day by coincidence. We stood in front of a green fence to have our photograph taken. A stranger, also wearing green, joined us.

Obsessed
Thank You Selena McKenzie

Camouflage
Picture of the Week

Camouflage
Thank You Benoit Santiard

Tires and TVs
Picture of the Week

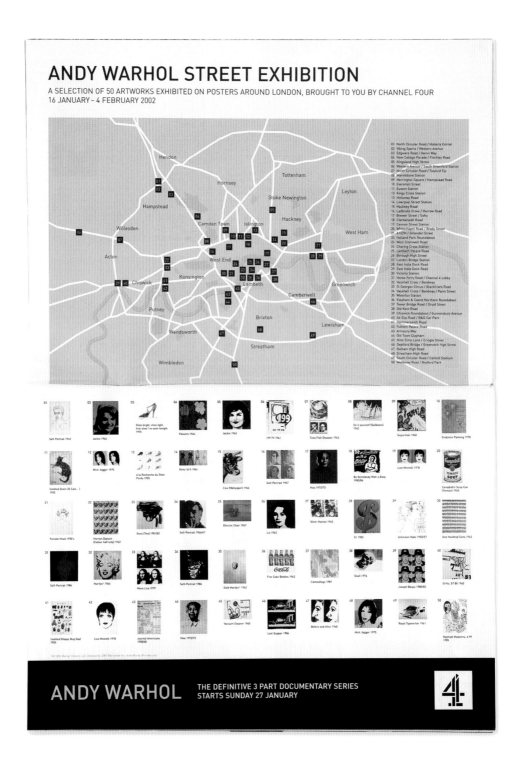

In 2002 some enterprising company erected fifty new square billboards in premium sites across London. Channel 4 bought all fifty. This made sense because the new format, which had the same surface area as a standard horizontal billboard but was square, connected to the number four and thus the Channel 4 logo. Channel 4 was the only advertiser using this new format.

Unlike the old method of screen-printing billboards, this new format is digitally printed on large tarpaulins, allowing each billboard to have a different design with no extra production cost.

To promote a three-part documentary about Andy Warhol in 2002, each of the fifty billboards displayed a different artwork of Warhol's, forming a street exhibition. An exhibition guide was inserted in newspapers and Time Out magazine, providing the locations of all the billboards in London. You can find photos of the billboards scattered throughout this book.

Self-Portrait, 1986
Vauxhall Cross/Bondway/Parry Street

$1, 1982
East India Dock Road

Protest House Signs
Picture of the Week

Reflection
Picture of the Week

The composite Christmas tree depicted on the front of this Christmas card was created by overlaying four drawings by my Mum, Dad, sister, and me, shown individually on the inside of the card.

Each drawing is printed with a 25 percent tint of black. When two lines overlap, the density increases to 50 percent; when three lines overlap, the density increases to 75 percent; and when all four lines overlap, the area becomes 100 percent black.

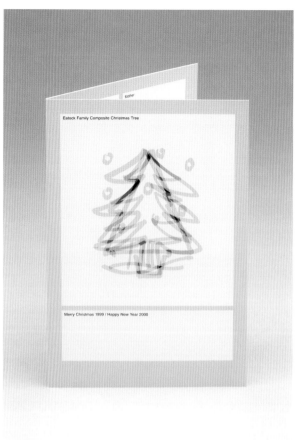

A laser printer containing a new toner cartridge was set to constantly print a black A4 document until the toner ran empty and a pure white sheet emerged, unprinted. As the pages exited the printer, I stacked them face up. The completed stack of paper contains the entire contents of the toner cartridge. The bottom page is black, the top page is white, and between is the transition—demise, depletion, expiration—from black to blank, full to empty.

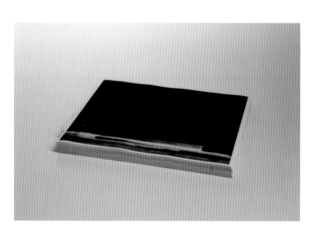

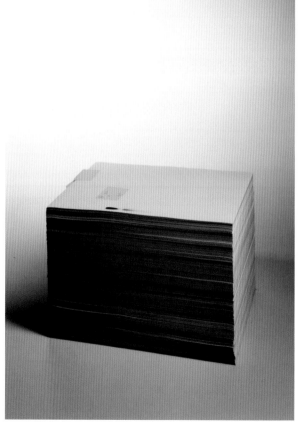

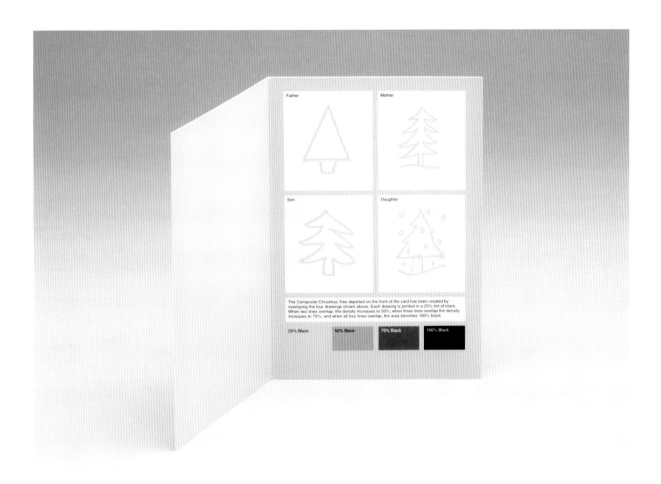

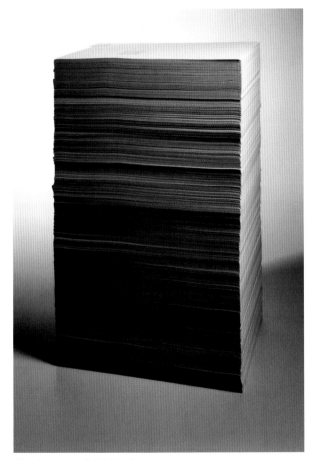

Final stack of 4,355 sheets

Half Step
Picture of the Week

Gargoyle
Picture of the Week

Boymeetsgirl
Single
Dating
Engaged
Married
Divorced
Desperate

159-173 St John Street
London EC1V 4RS

T 020 70126000
F 020 70126001
www.bmglondon.com

Our identity

The name of our company is
always written as one word.
The first letter (B) is always
capitalised.

The chosen typeface is
Akzidenz Grotesk Medium.

The new identity consists
of the following three
components:

1. Name
2. List of information
3. Pie chart

Boymeetsgirl is preceded with
a list of words coloured coded
to relate to a pie chart that
accurately summarises each
employees preference relating
to a topic.

The list and pie chart
represents each individuals
preferences, to form the
collective personality of the
company.

The topics are taken from
typical questionnaires and
relate to subjects individuals
discuss when introducing
themselves.

Summary

Boymeetsgirl's identity is
a collective summary of
each individuals personal
introduction.

The Questionnaire

Following are ten topics of
information.

You are asked to select
one preference from each
topic that most accurately
represents you.

A blank space has been left in
some instances where you are
able to specify another option.

Identity Questionnaire
001
Friday 3 December 2004

> Male
> Female
> Transsexual

> Single
> Dating
> Engaged
> Married
> Divorced
> Widowed
> Desperate

> English
> Irish
> Scottish
> Swedish
>

> 0-25
> 25-30
> 30-40
> 40-60
> 60+
> Unknown

> Gay
> Straight
> Bi
> Undecided
> Closet

> Dyslexic
> Allergic
> Diabetic
> Schizophrenic
> Impaired vision
> Deaf
> Blind
> Perfect
>

> Sleepy
> Grumpy
> Dopey
> Happy
> Bashful
> Sneezy
> Doc

> Right handed
> Left handed
> Ambidextrous

> Pessimist
> Optimist

> Mac
> PC

> Capricorn
> Aquarius
> Pisces
> Aries
> Taurus
> Gemini
> Cancer
> Leo
> Virgo
> Libra
> Scorpio
> Sagittarius

Please use the reverse of
this sheet to suggest other
categories and topics for
future questioners.

Eg. football teams, favourite
colour, pizza choice, etc.

Legal

This information is being
collected and used solely for
the purpose of the corporate
identity of Boymeetsgirl.

Your response to the
questionnaire will be
destroyed once the data has
been collected.

All information will be
collected on an anonymous
basis.

Questionnaire

Boymeetsgirl Democratic Graphic Identity

Created in 2005, the identity is a collective
summary of each staff member's personal
information, as compiled from a questionnaire.
A different set of information is contained on
each item of stationery.

Boymeetsgirl
Sleepy
Grumpy
Dopey
Happy
Bashful
Sneezy
Doc

Fourth Floor
159-173 St John Street
London EC1V 4RS

T 020 7012 6000
F 020 7012 6001
www.bmglondon.com

Compliment slip

Boymeetsgirl
English
Irish
Swedish
Other

Fourth Floor
159-173 St John Street
London EC1V 4RS

T 020 7012 6000
F 020 7012 6001
www.bmglondon.com

Boy Meets Girl LLP Reg. in England
No. OC308414 VAT No. GB 850 956616

Invoice

Boymeetsgirl
Sleepy
Dating
Engaged
Married
Co-habiting
Divorced

Fourth Floor
159-173 St John Street
London EC1V 4RS

T 020 7012 6000
F 020 7012 6001
www.bmglondon.com

Boy Meets Girl LLP Reg. in England No. OC308414

Letterhead

156

DL Envelope

Purchase order

Bar Chart

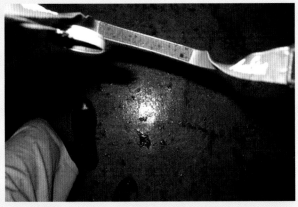

Camera Strap
Zakary Jensen

Bar Chart Grids
Picture of the Week

Untitled

Waiting in Line
Picture of the Week

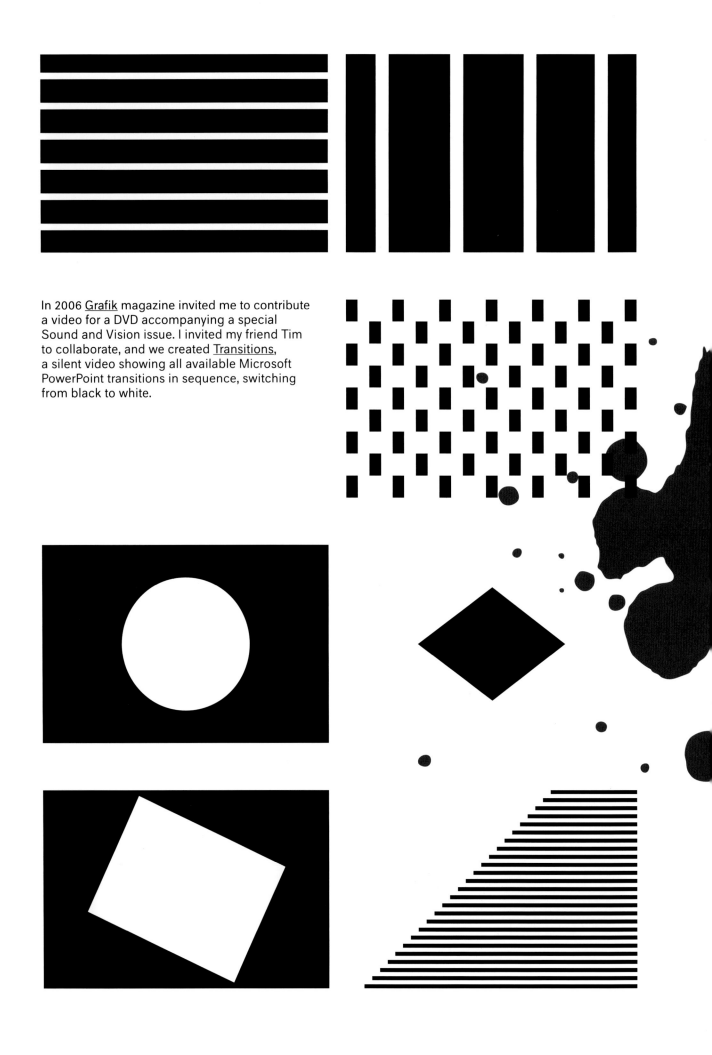

In 2006 Grafik magazine invited me to contribute a video for a DVD accompanying a special Sound and Vision issue. I invited my friend Tim to collaborate, and we created Transitions, a silent video showing all available Microsoft PowerPoint transitions in sequence, switching from black to white.

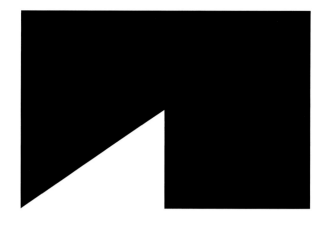

Expansion and Reduction

After viewing Transitions, I remembered a Quicktime video I had seen on an avant-garde art website. The film was Hans Richter's Rhythms 21, from 1921. The two films are quite similar at times, as both feature wipes from white to black and black to white. I found it interesting that there could be these parallels between works made eighty-five years apart, but although they occasionally appear similar, the films couldn't be further apart conceptually. Transitions is composed of reductions. Content, duration, and sequence are reduced to their simplest form by using the structure of the PowerPoint software. On the other hand, Rhythms 21 is about expansion. Previous to the creation of Richter's movie, the art of film had been pictorial, almost classical, compared to what was happening in the other arts. When Richter removed the actors and scenes that ordinarily dominate film he expanded the notions of film, painting, and, generally, visual art. Transitions reduces the visual overload we now live with to its most basic elements. In my opinion, both films make a clear statement on their respective time periods. They are like two points traveling on the same spiral—one inwards and one outwards.

(Derek Maxwell)

Precise and Professional
Thank You Ian Bolton

Stop, Wet Feet
Picture of the Week

Before and After, 1960
Balham High Road

Giraffe
Picture of the Week

159

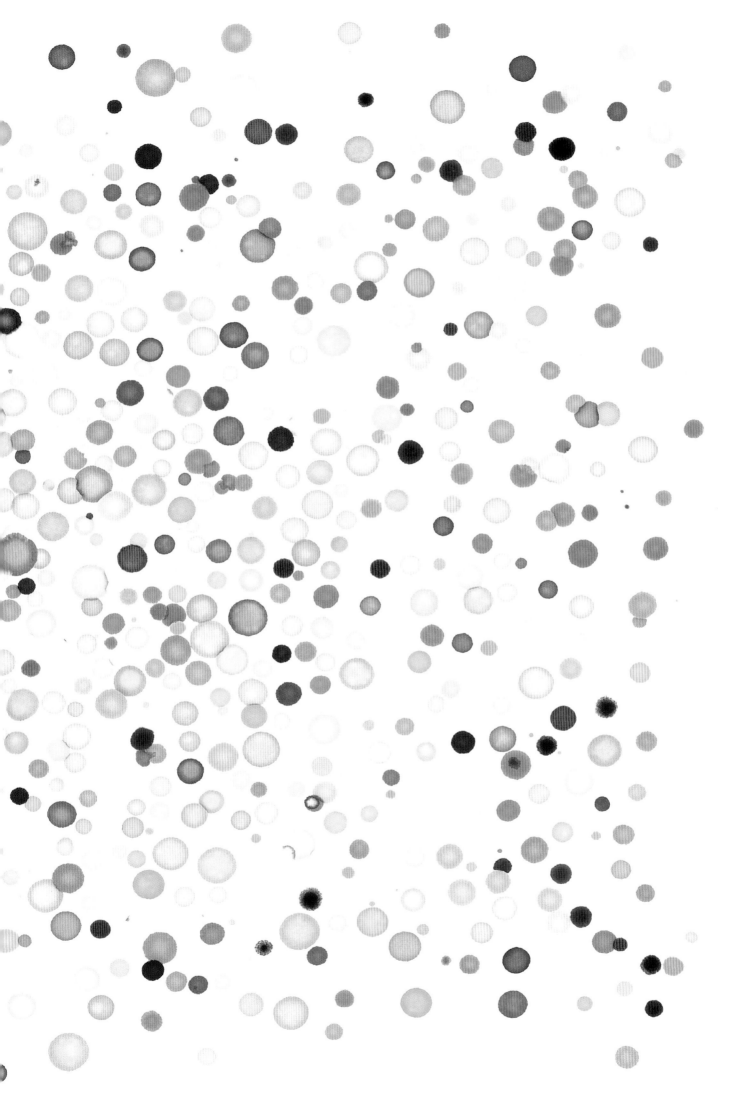

E Sketch
Shashi Pancholi

Felt-Tip Print was made by repeatedly balancing
a single A1 sheet of paper on the nibs of a set of
Pantone pens.

Green & Purple
Thank You Michael Jack

Matching Bag
Thank You Olivier Huz

Marilyn Diptych*(using only the color half of the original artwork), 1962
Holland Park Roundabout

E4 Big Brother logo

Fake Press Release

E4 has defaced and almost completely obliterated
the beautifully crafted Big Brother logo, spattering
it with paint, puke, vomit, spunk, blood, spit, and
ink. A Channel 4 spokesperson said, "E4 hijacked
and vandalized the iconic logo, showing total
disrespect, breaking all the rules, and creating
mayhem with their typical 'Fuck It' attitude."

Art
Picture of the Week

Purple Painting
Picture of the Week

For a billboard advertising the Turner Prize 2001, I duplicated the Channel 4 logo in every color contained in the identity style guide, retaining the logo's specified size in relation to the billboard format. The pattern is reminiscent of Andy Warhol's repetition, Damien Hirst's spots, and an artist's color palette.

Nearly all company identities have a corporate color: Coke red, IBM blue, and so on. Due to different print processes and materials, it is usually a constant nightmare to get accurate color-matching across different applications.

For Formation Architects' new identity I proposed the color green—all kinds of green. From the entire color spectrum, green is the color of which the human eye can distinguish the most variants. I designed printed stationery, report covers, and signage all in different greens. Employees chose their favorite hue of green for their business card. Almost all items of office supplies—bins, pencil sharpeners, rulers, folders—are available in green. Inevitably, these greens all differ and extend the identity. By slowly embracing green—building a library of green books for the reception area, assembling a collection of green bikes for employees, collecting a variety of green chairs— the firm generated an identity, whose variety creates a powerful unity that echoes the practice's diversity and environmentally aware outlook.

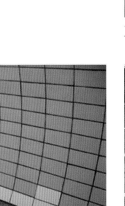

A set of invitations for a show curated by Flávia called Examining My Own Practise. The show presented performative works by six artists in relation to Flávia's own performance works. There was a personalized A6 postcard for each artist and a composite A5 postcard for Flávia that combined the six individual postcards to represent the complete show.

The set of seven postcards, six A6 and one A5, all fit perfectly on an SRA3 sheet of paper.

White Cloud
Picture of the Week

Low Clouds
Thank You Anthony Burrill

Ream of Litter
Picture of the Week

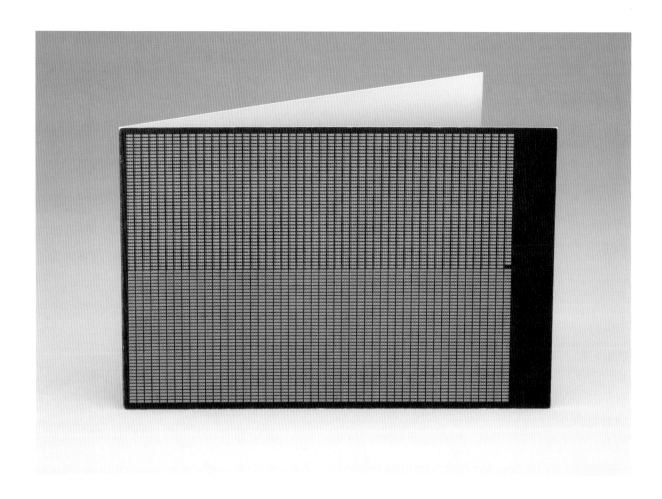

One of the last projects I did while working at the Walker Art Center was the 1999–2000 holiday card. I created a pattern by repeating the number 1999 one thousand nine hundred and ninety-nine times, and the number 2000 two thousand times. The difference between the two numbers is one, which is indicated by a small blank space.

When brought together, the two repeated blocks of digits had slightly different patterns, creating a subtle visual transition to the new millennium.

Bonsai

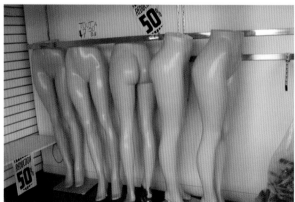

50% Reduction
Thank You Gail Trowbridge

Queue Gardens
Thank You Mark Ferguson

Pole Plant
Thank You Alfred Strik Swages

Mini-Me Tree
Thank You Anna Fidalgo

Upside-Down Tree
Picture of the Week

Similar Typefaces

Considered Graffiti
Picture of the Week

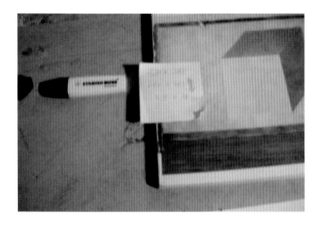
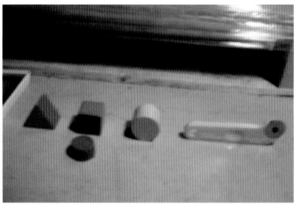

I was invited to give a one-week workshop at the Werkplaats Typografie in Arnhem, the Netherlands in 2005. At the end of the week, a few of the participants started to make impromptu connections between objects found in the studio. It started accidentally, when Jeff Ramsey, one of the participants, showed me a typeface he designed based on a font discovered on the cover of an old green book. Since making the font, he had found an almost identical one used on a twelve-inch record. This observation started a cascade of connections (the colors on the record cover matched those on a box of drinking chocolate), and the search for more began to form a trail of similarities, with color, form, and material linking one object to the next.

We filmed the trail on a digital camera in a dark studio, lighting each part with an Angle Poise lamp on a very long extension lead. The work was influenced by and connects to both Ryan Gander's "Loose Association" lecture and to the CD cover for Momus's Otto Spooky, designed by James Goggin. Five short Quicktime videos present the trail in its entirety. When viewed together, new connections and juxtapositions are formed between the five movies.

Thanks to the following collaborators from the Werkplaats workshop: Jeff Ramsey, David Bennewith, and Enrico Bravi.

John John John
Thank You Timothy Evans

Coming Down

Getting a Lift
Thank You Melvin Galapon

Transported Trailer
Picture of the Week

Wheel Rack
Picture of the Week

In 2005 I was commissioned by the <u>New York Times</u> to create three illustrations based on archetypal color-test charts to accompany a text by Kenji Yoshino titled, "Covering: The Hidden Assault on Our Civil Rights."

I worked on this project at the same time as the <u>Felt-Tip Print</u>. I felt overwhelmed by dots.

<u>E Sketch</u>
Gillian McDermott

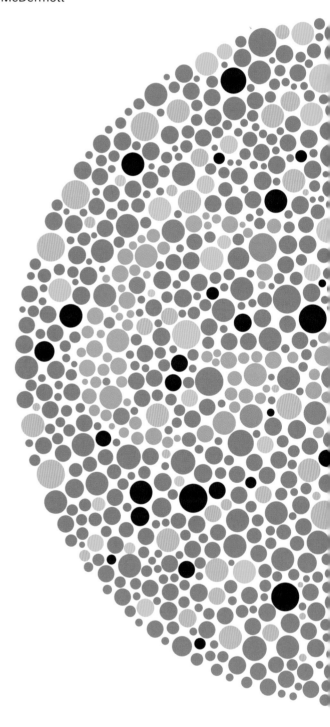

Audio Visual

1. Arrange an amplifier and a slide
projector so they are directly
facing each other.

2. Fill the slide projector's carousel
with slides taken of the amplifier.

3. Run a microphone from the amplifier
and place it on the top of the slide
carousel.

4. Turn the amplifier on at full
volume and run the slide projector
on constant projection.

The slide projector will project
the amplifier at the amplifier, and
the amplifier will project the sound
of the slide projector at the slide
projector. The audio and visual
function in perfect harmony.

Ink Bleed

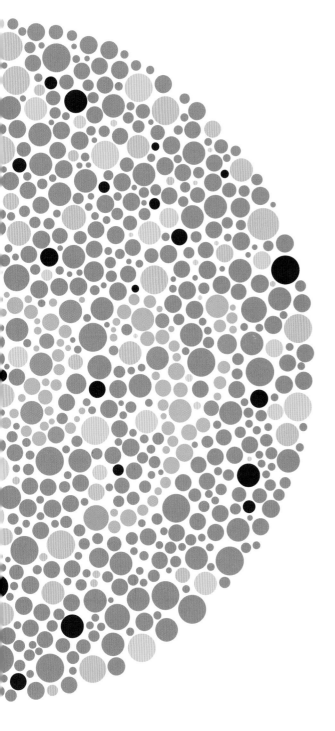

Blue Spot Blue Top
Picture of the Week

Echo
Picture of the Week

Ink Bleed

Perfect

Perfect

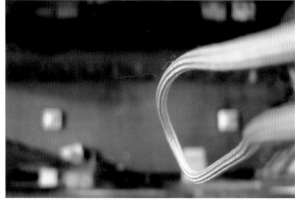

Camera Strap
Peter Clarkson

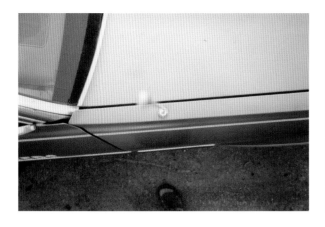

Perfect

Aerial Views

I stretched out my arm and held my camera directly above the top of these car aerials (antennas) attempting to take a perfect aerial view.

Color-Coordinated Clamp Stripe
Picture of the Week

Camouflaged Bike Components
Picture of the Week

Camera Strap
Denis Lirette

Ballpoint Removed

In response to an invitation from Pentagram
partner Angus Hyland in 2004 to create a work that
uses a ballpoint pen, I removed the ballpoint from
a pen and taped the ink reservoir directly to the
gallery wall, allowing the ink to run slowly down
the wall and create a thick line of dark blue ink.

Exhibited as part of the group show Ball Point in
the Pentagram Gallery.

Camo Lock
Picture of the Week

E Sketch
Bill Hewlett

Volcano
Picture of the Week

Using an Edding 0.1 pen, I placed a single dot in the center of each millimeter square on an A1 sheet of graph paper.

I designed this sticker sheet for my friend Louise, who is a filmmaker. She had just graduated from the Royal College of Art and needed a cheap and flexible set of stationary.

The design is based on the sheets of stickers that come with VHS tapes. I have always liked the half-used sheets and the blank spaces that are left after some of the stickers have been removed.

The identity stickers require a creative application to blank paper, cards, envelopes, packages, and tapes. They can be arranged in many combinations, forming a flexible identity that connects and unifies many disparate elements.

I asked Louise to always include the remaining sticker sheet with the object to which she had applied the removed stickers.

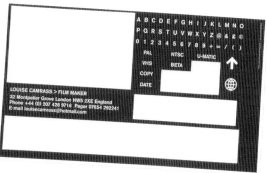

Grass Flags
Thank You Simon Jones

Tottenham Court Road Deforestation
Picture of the Week

Every Punch Made by My Hole Punch
(see next spread)
Ongoing project

Flower
Picture of the Week

Mail and Femail

WALKER ART CENTER

THEATER

SPEAK BITTERNESS

FORCED ENTERTAINMENT

$16 ($6 WALKER MEMBERS)

WALKER ART CENTER
VINELAND PLACE
at Lyndale Avenue South
MINNEAPOLIS, MN 55403

MARCH 11 – 13
THURSDAY @ 8pm
✳ FRIDAY @ 9:30 pm
SATURDAY @ 8pm

WALKER ART CENTER
AUDITORIUM

612-375-7622
(TDD: 612-375-7585)
Patrons with special needs are asked to call two weeks in advance. Tickets may be purchased in advance to all Walker events (subject to availability).

"BRITAIN'S MOST BRILLIANT EXPERIMENTAL COMPANY." THE GUARDIAN

British theater iconoclasts FORCED ENTERTAINMENT make a rare and brief U.S. tour to present their latest work, SPEAK BITTERNESS. Strange and comical, chaotic and cathartic, the work draws on the cultures of confession witnessed in contemporary talk shows, churches, and national scandals. SPEAK BITTERNESS is a riveting and intimate piece that pulls the audience in and introduces them to seven nicely dressed penitents whose task is to confess everything ranging from large-scale failings such as

✳ 50% off with AFTER HOURS ticket stub. FRIDAY ONLY

www.walkerart.org
© 1999 Walker Art Center

Nonprofit Organization
U.S. Postage
PAID
MINNEAPOLIS, MN
Permit Number 3213

forgery or genocide to those nasty little details like reading each others diaries.

A5 invitation card

Too Big?
Thank You Jeffery Bennett

Wet Paint Advertisement
Picture of the Week

Keep
Picture of the Week

<u>Word Sculptures</u>

Table topless
Television aerial view
Tie a rainbow
Tin can't
Toilet rolling pin
Tooth pick axe
Train tractor
Train track suit
Washing machine gun
Waterfall over
Angry crossword
Autographed signpost
Baby sitting down
Barbecue up
Birthday credit card
Boat deck chair
Book reserved
Bowtie and arrow
Brand newspaper
Burning fireman
Camera film star
Clean washing line
Computer disco
Computer mouse trap
Cowboy udder
Cricket batman
Crying whale

Daffodil light bulb
Dandelion tamer
Dark light shade
Divorced stepladder
Door key board
Engine and tonic
Femail box
Filofax machine
Gate postbox
Girlfriendly
Goalpostcard
Half price yacht sale
Hammer toenail
Heavy light switch
High-rise flat
Ill wishing well
Khaki car key
Lazy bulldozer
Mad cowboy disease
Melted butterfly
Microwave goodbye
Navy sealed envelope
Newspaper hat
Pencil knife
Plain aeroplane
Plastic iron
Postcardboard
Bifocal wine glasses
Quick breakfast

The beginning of
The Art Show

1

Exclusive for everybody
The Art Show

2

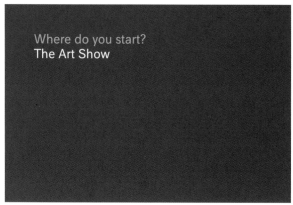

Where do you start?
The Art Show

3

Not just about art
The Art Show

4

Radio controlled radio
Flat battery hen
Right hand gliding
Santa's sledge hammer
Short brief case
Sinking space ship
Soup bowling
Stationary bus stop
Suitable suit
Sun settee
Swimming tree trunks

£1 Field Recording

1. Using a ten-pence piece, dial
your answering machine from a public
telephone.

2. Let the answering machine record
any ambient sounds for the duration
of the ten-pence piece.

3. Repeat step one and two ten times
from ten different locations.

The total duration of the piece will
depend on the location and time of
each call.

Mobile Phone Performance/Lecture

Please leave your mobile phone on.
If your phone rings, answer and inform
the caller that you are in a lecture.
The duration of the performance will
be one hour and fifteen minutes. I
will silently present a portfolio of
projects. I will play music from my
iPod on "shuffle." I will take questions
via my mobile phone. I will be silent
unless answering a question.

For the performance to progress, it
is necessary that you ask questions.

I will skip forward to another track
if I don't like a particular song.
If the discussion gets boring, please
call and interrupt. I will be editing
the questions and only answering
good ones.

My number is +44 (0)7811 177965

Thursday, 13 November 2003
Central Saint Martins
College of Art and Design
Cochran Theatre, London

Accommodating Brick
Picture of the Week

Talking Behind Their Backs
Thank You Sarah Gottlieb

Male and Female
Picture of the Week

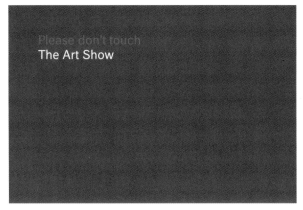

Please don't touch
The Art Show

5

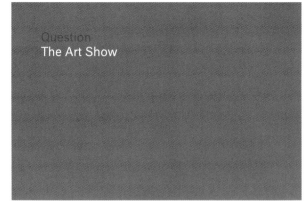

Question
The Art Show

6

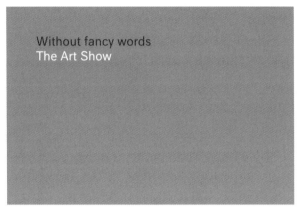

Without fancy words
The Art Show

7

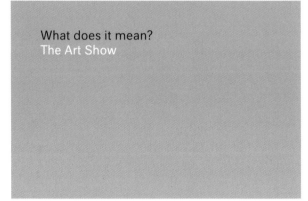

What does it mean?
The Art Show

8

Interpret
The Art Show

9

Ends in 30 minutes

10

This is a title sequence for The Art Show, a ten-part program about contemporary art, design, and culture shown on Channel 4 in 2002.

The title sequence lasts for ten seconds, during which the background fades from black to white and the subtitles fade from white to black (opposite to background), creating a halfway transition as both the type and background colors momentarily appear as 50 percent black. The title of the show remains white and appears to dissolve as the background fades to white.

Matching Parking Fine
Thank You Michael Craven

White Blackboard

In the coffee bar at the Royal College of Art a large blackboard covers one wall, which is used to write down pool game scores, jokes, messages, doodles, and graffiti. My friend Martin Anderson and I decided to color the entire blackboard white using regular sticks of chalk. It took us the entire day, with the help of a few friends during their coffee breaks.

Matching Parking Fine
Picture of the Week

Black Blackboard
Picture of the Week

Table Mat

In early 2008 I was invited by Sara Ludvigsson, a curator in Stockholm, to create an artwork for a table mat. The mat, printed in an edition of two thousand, was exhibited at Riche, a posh restaurant in Stockholm, for one month. Guests were allowed to keep the mats when they left the restaurant.

Dead Man's Cup

When my Mum and Dad were having some building work done recently, my Mum made tea and coffee for the workers, using a set of odd cups rather than her best china. Two weeks later she found out that one of the builders had died. This is the cup he drank from, now known as "dead man's cup."

Two hundred identical cups for an office of two hundred people.

E Sketch
James Haggerty

From 2000 to 2004 I was the third-year graphic design teacher at the University of Brighton. At lunchtime I would often walk down to the beach and look out at the ocean. One day I bought a cheap glass from a catering supply shop and walked down to the beach to collect a glass of seawater. I attempted to fill the glass from the sea without getting my feet wet—impossible. I walked into the sea and scooped up a full glass of seawater and a few pebbles before I returned to the college with wet shoes, socks, and jeans. I spent the whole afternoon giving tutorials with wet feet.

At the end of the day, I carefully carried the glass—without a lid—all the way back to my apartment in London, using the train and the London Underground. I held the glass constantly, using my arm as a kind of suspension shock-absorbing device to limit the amount of spillage. I managed to bring almost a full glass back, with only about twenty millimeters of seawater lost. I placed the glass at the side of my bed and watched as it slowly evaporated over the next few weeks, leaving behind beautiful salt crystals.

Coffee Color Match
Picture of the Week

Bikini Beach
Picture of the Week

Stop, Wait, and Go
Thank You James Greenfield

Stop, Wait, and Go
Thank You Vicky Simmons

Stop, Wait, and Go
Thank You Nick Evans

Stop, Wait, and Go
Thank You Lemoine Benoit

Stop, Wait, and Go
Thank You Simon Jones

Stop, Wait, and Go
Thank You Pierre Leguillon

Stop, Wait, and Go
Thank You Simon Jones

Stop, Wait, and Go
Thank You Sarah Gottlieb

Stop, Wait, and Go

Stop, Wait, and Go

Stop Go Bags
Picture of the Week

Stop, Wait, and Go

White Cloud at Sunset
Picture of the Week

I don't like the subjectivity associated with composition. My <u>Sun Light</u> pictures have a rationalized, semiobjective aesthetic—there is only one viewpoint from which the picture can be taken. I positioned myself so the street lamp eclipsed the sun and centered the sun in the picture.

<u>Bikini</u>
Thank You Andrea Amato

<u>Pink Proud</u>
Picture of the Week

<u>Flying Saucer</u>
Picture of the Week

Designers, painters, and photographers often
refer to an image, page, or form as looking
"balanced"—a subjective description suggesting
that the image, page, or form appears comfortable
and harmonious. The elements are not too heavy
or lopsided, but equally spaced.

Everybody remembers being a child and leaning
back on only two legs of a chair. A special
sensation is created when the body is suspended
momentarily, neither falling forward nor backward.
The moment the chair inches back, the body
reacts by throwing legs and arms forward to
counterbalance, resulting in a feeling of butterflies
in your stomach.

Skateboarders, surfers, tightrope walkers, trials
riders and unicyclists are constantly teetering
on the edge of balance, with movement and
momentum keeping them from falling. Subtle
movements and adjustments are required
to stay in control. These are often twitchy and
seemingly erratic, yet they are intuitive reactions
to maintain balance.

Balance is the striving for stillness created by
the constant adjustments and movements that
bracket the point of balance.

New Bike

194

Microphone Vacuum Suck

2 Tables for 1 Outside
Thank You Steve Lea

Kissing Ketchup
Picture of the Week

Tricycle
Thank You Maxime Delporte

~~Run-Over-Cycle Lane~~ / Unicycle Lane
Picture of the Week

Made by linking archetypal silver clasps, <u>Neckclasp</u> subverts the typical notions of beauty by allowing the functional element of a necklace, normally concealed at the back of the wearer's neck, to be highlighted and used as the single component that forms the piece.

<u>Neckclasp</u> can be fastened or unfastened at any point along its length and celebrates the frustrating problem of the clasp working its way to the limelight at the front.

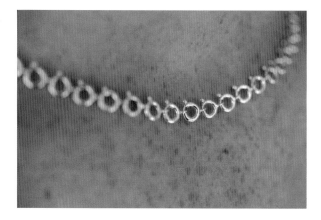

Dear Daniel,

Yesterday I saw your necklace "Neckclasp" on your Internet site. I think you didn't know that I have this design in my collection since 1989 under the name "Missing Link" in gold and silver. This chain is published several times since then and if you are interested you can see it in my book which is published by Arnoldsche Publishers "HermanHermsen: Jewelry, Light and More."

So please think about what you can decide.

nice greetings,

Herman Hermsen

PS. My website is in construction so if you want to see more of my works, you can look to the pictures under my name in Google.

Hello Herman,

It seems that we have used the same idea. I am not sure what to do. When I first had the idea, I checked and asked many people if they had seen it before. I felt it was a very obvious thing that somebody must have made, but I found nothing. I gave one to Flávia, my wife, as a present, then did nothing for five years. I only showed a photo of the prototype on my old website, http://www.foundation33.com. Then, about a year ago, I decided to work with TRICO to manufacture and sell it. It is a really nice project, and I like how the object and title connect.

What would you like me to do? It seems you got to the idea first. The emphasis of my practice is to invent. I hate when people copy or use ideas.

Awaiting your reply.

Best,

Dan

Hi Daniel,

Thank you for your kind and honest answer to my mail. Most ideas come spontaneously out of a conceptional thinking and fit completely perfect to the identity of the collection of work. Unfortunately some ideas do exist already. It also happened to me several times and is a great pity and an unpleasant feeling, especially when there is an investment of work, energy, and money.

But in those cases I withdraw my design, so there is no conflict and no irritation on the market, because the contemporary jewelry scene is very small and a name is ruined very quickly.

I made the "missing link" first for an exhibition at gallery V+V in Vienna in 1989 and after that I distributed it to galleries in USA, Germany, Netherlands, Japan, Belgium, Portugal, Italy and to a museum collection in the Netherlands and Germany.

It is very unpleasant for you to stop the project, but it is wise in a way, that you keep your name clean.

Nice greetings,

Herman

Hello Herman,

Thank you for your e-mail. I feel I have a very different interest in the work. I am not a jewelry designer. I enjoy taking existing things—readymade, archetypal objects—and forming something new. I feel that the title I gave the piece is of equal importance to the object as the object itself.

It is one of many works of mine where the title and object connect. I shall leave the work on my website and continue selling it via TRICO. I will not present it at jewelry fairs, sell it in jewelry shops, or publish it in jewelry press.

I feel confident that because of the nature of the work, people will understand that two people independently connected the clasps together to make two separate works.

Best regards,

Dan

Hello Daniel,

OK, let's stick to that, and as you say you will sell it only via Trico. I looked at their site and it is an interesting collection of very different designers. A good company, I suppose.

Wish you success with your developments and art.

Best regards,

Herman

Trapped Superhero
Picture of the Week

Kabab Loop
Picture of the Week

Camera Strap
Ben Little

Camera Strap
Eli Rikter-Svendsen

Camera Strap
Malcolm Chivers

Removed Sticker

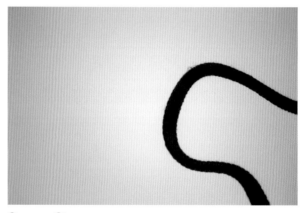

Camera Strap
Mat Jones

Camera Strap
Caro Mikalef

Depressed Street Sign
Thank You Ilona Hansson

In a Flap in Croydon
Thank You Andrew Sturt

Big Brother billboard with public intervention

Untitled
Thank You Caroline Andram

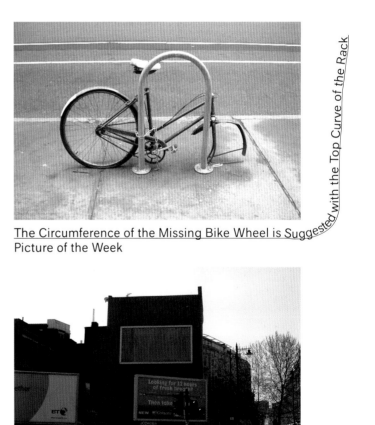

The Circumference of the Missing Bike Wheel is Suggested with the Top Curve of the Rack
Picture of the Week

Fly Poster
Thank You Kirsty Carter

Ply Ad
Picture of the Week

Numerical Time-Based Sound Composition

A digital time display counts up to one hour using four units: seconds, tens of seconds, minutes, and tens of minutes.

A numerical sound composition was constructed using the ten sequential digits: 0, 1, 2, 3, 4, 5, 6, 7, 8, 9. Each digit was assigned a tone. The tones were mathematically selected from the range of twenty to twenty thousand hertz: the two extremes audible to the human ear. The tones were logarithmically divided between the ten digits, providing tonal increments that produced a musical scale.

Every second, a different combination of four tones is defined by the time counter. Above is a diagram that represents the hour-long composition.

Composer: Daniel Eatock
Musician: Timothy Evans

Bust in for a Piss
Thank You Greg Hardes

Camera Strap
Sebastian Greenall

Dan came to me with a basic thought about an audio piece. The project's seed was planted in one of Jon Wozencroft's seminars on sound at the Royal College of Art. Imagine a dull classroom full of bright students being subjected to the more abstract reaches of audio art: it was easy for one's mind to wander. Dan's eyes became focused on the only movement in the room: the CD player's digital time counter. He became interested in the way the repetitive sounds occasionally aligned with the ticking of the CD counter. This reminded me of when, as a child, I was stuck in a rainy traffic jam. I became interested in how the repetitive movement of the windshield wipers went in and out of phase with the flashing car indicators. Dan asked, "Why not write a musical score driven by, and perfectly in time with, the CD time counter?" It could be a dog's bark each time the number five appeared, a whistle for number six, and so on.

When we started working together, we agreed some further rational decisions were needed to strengthen the idea. Our excitement was in making a composition that was defined as closely as possible by the CD counter. Unlike most musical endeavors, we wanted our piece to be mathematically precise and thoroughly objective. A composition of one hour would fit onto a standard audio CD and use the full range of the time counter. Instead of random sounds, we felt something more pure and basic was needed. There are four spaces on the time display. Over an hour, you can see how ten digits are used to describe the current time. We chose to use ten different frequencies, one for each digit. The frequencies span the human range of hearing.

A friend figured out the math required to define the frequencies. Using a computer, the sixty-minute composition was relatively easy to construct. Unlike previous sound projects we had made, this piece was recorded on CD without us even listening to it all the way through. After putting the disc in the CD player, we found the idea worked perfectly. Each time a digit ticked over, the frequency stepped on one notch. There are always four layers of sound, and you can hear some odd effects as frequencies combine and collide. We hope the cover design is equally pragmatic. Similar to the computer timeline from the audio program with which the composition was constructed, shades of gray represent the varying frequencies. This project attempts to remove subjective expression from the music-making process. It takes a simple idea and pushes it to logical extremes. The systematic approach functions in both audio and visual terms. In the completed project, it seems the visual could never be separated from the audio.

(Timothy Evans)

Free Bench
Thank You Adam Hayes

Imprisoned Bench
Picture of the Week

Vorsprung Durch Technik
Thank You Benji Wiedemann

Measured Up
Picture of the Week

Dandruff scan with black background

Dandruff scan with white background

E Sketch
Lydia Abastado

Talking Tree
Thank You David Darnes

Virgin Mary
Thank You Kris McCaddon

Balloon Blow

Giant Grapes
Thank You David Oscroft

Balloon Bush
Picture of the Week

Opposites
Thank You Rory Gleeson

Jeff Koons Puppies, Bilbao
Picture of the Week

I created the <u>Design Department Internship Poster</u>, made to promote the Walker Art Center's internship program and find our future replacements, in collaboration with my fellow intern Erin Mulcahy. The two-sided poster represents every project produced during the first six months of our internships at the Walker.

Every page of each project is shown front and back. The result registers the scope of our production in literal terms. This straightforward strategy of information display is countered by personal commentary linked to each project.

<u>Archetypal</u>
Postcard back composition

<u>Big Message Small Address</u>
Postcard back composition

<u>Small Message Big Address</u>
Postcard back composition

<u>Disjointed</u>
Postcard back composition

<u>Night of the Driving Red</u>
Thank You Ben Clarke

<u>Parked</u>
Thank You Becky Sinden

<u>Down Here</u>
Picture of the Week

<u>Triple Orange</u>
Thank You Tom Merrell

<u>Color-Coordinated Car</u>
Picture of the Week

A MUSEUM OF CONTEMPORARY VISUAL, PERFORMING, AND MEDIA ARTS.

APPLICANTS MUST HAVE AN INTEREST IN CONTEMPORARY ARTS AND CULTURAL TRENDS, MACINTOSH PROFICIENCY (QUARK, PHOTOSHOP, ILLUSTRATOR), EXCELLENT TYPOGRAPHIC SKILLS, EXPERIENCE WITH PRINT PRODUCTION, AND AN UNDERGRADUATE OR GRADUATE DEGREE IN GRAPHIC DESIGN.

THE TWELVE-MONTH, FULL-TIME INTERNSHIP BEGINS OCTOBER 1, 1999, AND CONCLUDES SEPTEMBER 30, 2000. THE SALARY IS $19,500 PLUS A $1,000 TRAVEL STIPEND AND EXCELLENT BENEFITS.

AN EQUAL OPPORTUNITY/AFFIRMATIVE ACTION EMPLOYER; WOMEN, PEOPLE OF COLOR, AND PEOPLE WITH DISABILITIES ARE ENCOURAGED TO APPLY.

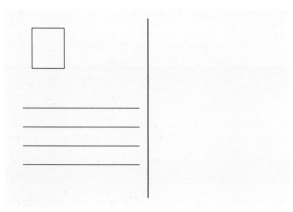

Opposite
Postcard back composition

E Sketch
John Brown

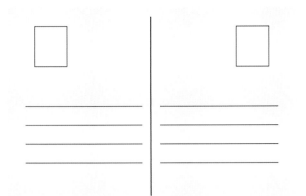

Reflected
Postcard back composition

FUTURE^TS

RTS Futures Logo
(Royal Television Society)

Hot Madonna
Thank You David Beesley

Double Take
Thank You Jordan Sheldrick

House Extension
Picture of the Week

Double Burger
Thank You Benoit Lemoine

Full Body
Picture of the Week

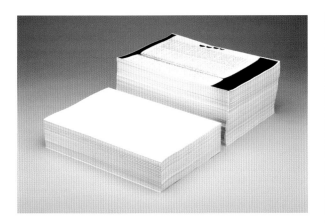

Tree Prison Two
Picture of the Week

I photocopied every page of the Concise Oxford English Dictionary onto A4 sheets of paper to produce a stack of more than fifteen hundred pages. This project was inspired by the fact that books are often photocopied for reference. The dictionary is the archetypal reference book. Photocopying it resulted in a handmade duplicate that has more value than the original due to the time and expense invested in making it. The height of the stack makes the volume of information contained in a dictionary—normally disguised by the thin weight of its paper—more tangible and gives it more weight physically and conceptually.

Complimentary Clamp
Picture of the Week

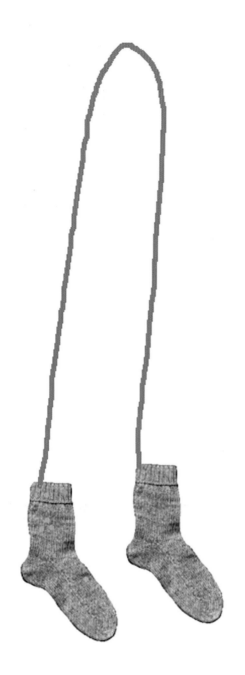

Camera Strap
Sophia Ben Yedder

Where's Stu?
Thank You Darren

Big & Little
Thank You Gavin Day

A string connecting a pair of socks goes up one trouser leg and down the other in reference to children's mittens.

Scissors Who Need Scissors to Use Them
Thank You Daniël Maarleveld

Loop

Man Dressed Like Shop
Thank You Ben Bateson

Double Parked
Thank You Ned Selby

Matching Socks
Thank You Philippe Egger

Camouflage
Thank You Brendan Lee

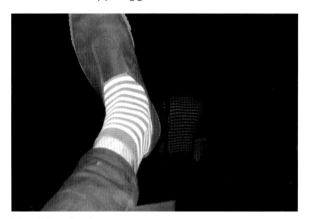

Matching Sock
Picture of the Week

Camouflage
Thank You Jaime Bishop

Tree Stump
Picture of the Week

Buried Treasure

One morning a worker dug a hole directly outside
my studio using a jackhammer. After a couple of
hours of making very loud noise, he went away
for lunch and left the hole. An hour later, he came
back and filled the hole in.

Sun Spot
Thank You David Parle

Gone Places
Thank You Chris Allard

Bad Pun Tempts Fate
Thank You David Coyle

Dead End
Thank You Christian Eager

Last Few Days
Thank You Gareth White

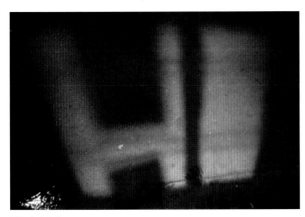

High Light
Thank You David Parle

Spot Light
Picture of the Week

E Sketch
Mark Mason

Bus Stop Stopped
Picture of the Week

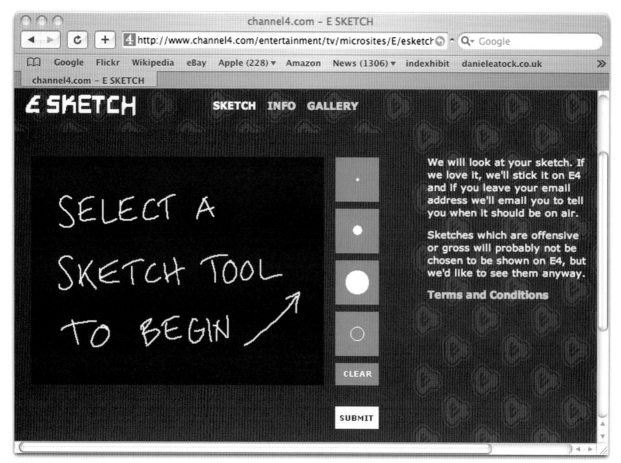

E Sketch www.channel4.com/esketch

While working on my pitch to create a new identity for Channel 4 in 2003, I became interested in how the channel's viewers could be a part of the process. Collaborating with Sara De Bondt, I proposed a simple drawing interface that would allow people to make and submit a drawing on the Channel 4 website. The best drawings would be selected to appear as part of the channel identity.

This idea turned out to be too democratic for Channel 4, but was perfect for its sister channel, E4. We worked with two programmers to build the drawing tool E Sketch, which can be found at www.channel4.com/esketch and enables anybody to create a sketch and send it to E4. A selection of E Sketches from the submissions go on air every week. The sketches are personal, political, topical, surreal, serious, irreverent, incredibly artistic, or very basic. Many relate back to E4 shows and characters, creating an interesting loop, with viewers commenting on and promoting the E4 shows. E Sketch has provided a platform for viewers to communicate to a huge audience and literally allows them to contribute to the channel's content.

All E Sketches received by E4 are reviewed; the best sketches are tagged and saved in a database, ready for broadcasting later that day. Each person is informed via e-mail when their sketch will be broadcast.

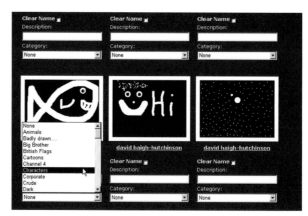

E Sketch curatorial interface

E Sketch
Roshan Meerun

214

E Sketch
Mel Lydiatt

E Sketch
Matthew Lowther

Pink Bra Pink Rubbish
Picture of the Week

Graffiti with Nothing to Say
Picture of the Week

A6 postcard

A6 postcard

A6 postcard

A6 postcard

From: Guilherme Falcão Pelegrino
Subject: Re: Interview

Tell me a bit about your postcards, such as "Email,"
"Private And Confidential," and "Junk Mail."

They remind me of that Magritte painting <u>Ceci n'est</u>
<u>pas une pipe</u>—not in the sense of representation
(this is not a pipe, but a pipe's representation),
but in how you say what something is, only to reaffirm
what it is. When you write "Private And Confidential,"
for instance. A postcard is anything but private
and confidential. It seems to me there is some irony
in the whole idea... at the same time as you're
denying what it is, you also make us think about
what it isn't.

A6 postcard

A6 postcard

A6 postcard

Return to Sender

A6 postcard

<u>Post Post</u>
Thank You Nigel Ball

<u>!!</u>
Thank You Sarah Gottlieb

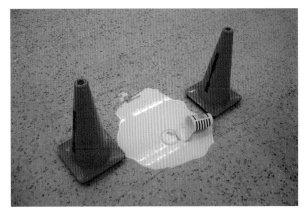

<u>Caution Cream</u>
Picture of the Week

<u>Confirmation</u>
Picture of the Week

WALKER ART CENTER VISUAL ARTS CURATORIAL INTERNSHIP OPPORTUNITIES 1999–2000

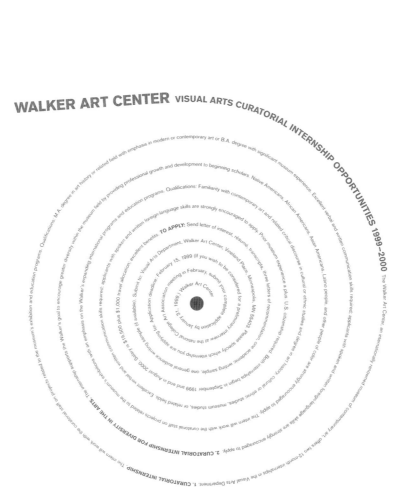

In 1999 I made a poster for the Walker Art Center to advertise for three visual arts interns. The poster is designed to be pinned to the wall with a pushpin in the center of the text spiral. The viewer has to turn the poster to read the information. The last word in the spiral is "Center." A red dot was hand-applied to the center of the spiral on each poster as a locating point for the pushpin.

Sunbathing
Thank You Gavin Day

In 2006 Tim Hall, a friend of Bill Griffin (the ex-marketing director of Channel 4), asked me to create a logo for his new sandwich shop, called Pod. There are not that many symmetrical words, so it made sense to embrace the name's symmetry. The logo is a circle that can be applied to coffee cups, sandwich bags, and salad boxes in any orientation. The more randomly it is applied, the better it looks.

Portrait
Postcard back composition

Double
Thank You Simon Jones

Side Street
Picture of the Week

Twin Twin
Thank You Nigel Ball

Four Black Bins and Four Black Garage Doors
Picture of the Week

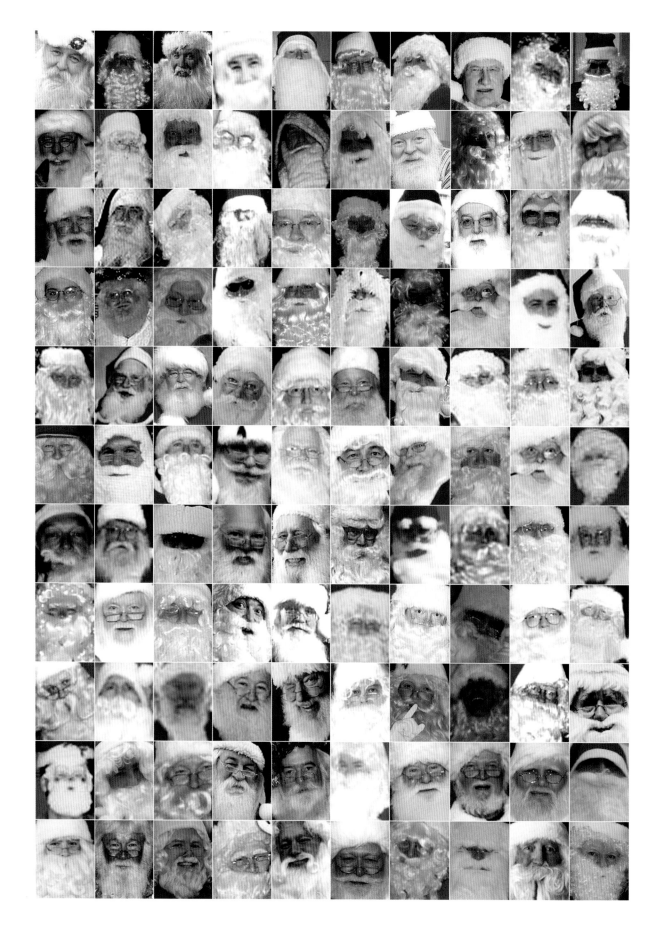

Real Santa

Humbug Christmas Card

Santa Self-Portrait
Picture of the Week

Winter and Summer
Picture of the Week

Camera Strap
Rik Moran

100 Greatest Films billboard 1

100 Greatest Films billboard 2

Channel 4 has a series of programs called 100 Greatest…. I was invited to make a tease-and-reveal billboard campaign to promote 100 Greatest Films. The first, "tease," billboard was all black, apart from the repetition of the Channel 4 logo to reference the leader edge of a strip of film. The "reveal" billboard is caught between two frames, emphasizing the physical movement of film.

E Sketch
Jade Corcoran

Camera Strap
Andrea Balzarini

Keyboard Catch

Superset logo

Tambourine Tennis Ball Bounce

Rirkrit Tiravanija book

Color-Coded Wheel Clamp
Picture of the Week

Microphone Stomp

Friends
Picture of the Week

223

Photography credits

Hein van Liempd
22, 23

Carlo Draisci
24, 25, 26, 28, 30, 34, 35, 38, 39, 44, 48, 49, 50, 51,
53, 56, 57, 65, 66, 68, 69, 75, 90, 91, 94, 96, 97, 98,
100, 102, 116, 118, 120, 122, 123, 126, 127, 137, 138, 139,
142, 143, 150, 152, 153, 154, 155, 160, 161, 163, 164,
165, 166, 167, 168, 177, 178, 179, 180, 181, 182, 183, 188,
196, 200, 209, 218, 221, 222, 223

Jérôme Saint-Loubert Bié
36, 37

David Grandorge
62, 63, 76, 77, 78, 98, 144, 147, 193

Donald Christie
90

Xavier Young
154, 156

Coffee Table

Big Winners (Gold, Silver, and Bronze)
Thank You Simon Jones

Saplings
Picture of the Week

Palette Francaise
Thank You Tom Henni

I would like to record the sound of a drill onto a CD that has no hole in the center.

I would like to stick a full role of masking tape in one long straight line and then keep adding new rolls below until the length of the unravelled roles is matched by the multiple line widths forming one enormous masking tape square.

I would like to put an Alka-Seltzer in a pint of beer.

I would like to have the very first photograph I ever took.

I would like to have seen Andy Kaufman read The Great Gatsby.

I would like to know how many names and spellings there are for all the countries in the European Union in the language of each country.

I would like to photograph frames, print them actual size on large sheets of paper, and hang them unframed on a wall.

I would like to take 35-mm slide transparencies of playground slides in various children's playgrounds and project them as a slide show.

I would like to ask people what they are going to buy as they are walking into a supermarket, and ask them what they bought when they come out.

I would like to make an archetypal steel ruler that is one kilometer long.

I would like to be asked to spell every word in the Concise Oxford English Dictionary as part of a standard high school spelling test. I would form a list of all the words I spelled wrong and a list of all the words I spelled correctly.

I would like to replace the word fragile that appears on hardback envelopes with the word delicate.

I would like to photograph the wounds that most designers have on their fingers as a result of using scalpels and form a picture book called Scalpel Scars.

I would like to curate a show called Untitled containing only works that are untitled.

I would like to buy postcards in art museums of artworks on display, hold them in front of the artworks, and photograph them.

I would like to design a football kit. The team members would all wear plain white T-shirts and stand in a line, while I walk around them spraying a continuous red line across the fronts and backs of their T-shirts.

I would like to be a husband.

I would like to spend a weekend with Rupert and Julie in their new country home.

I would like to make A1 box frames with a fifteen-centimeter-wide slot cut into the glass that would allow people to insert photographs into them.

I would like to own a complete set of Edward Ruscha's artist books.

I would like to get married to Flávia.

I would like to win the lottery and buy two weeks in a recording studio for Ween and Camper Van Beethoven to collaborate on an album.

I would like my living environment to be open to the public as a gallery and artwork.

I would like to have salamis hanging from the ceiling in my kitchen.

I would like to make more meals for friends.

I would like to cycle on the winding roads of the French Alps with my girlfriend Flávia on a lightweight tandem.

I would like to have more outdoor barbecues.

I would like to collaborate with 3M and make the Fly Post-it an artwork that is manufactured by a huge multinational organization.

I think that Jackass star Steve-O's tattoo, spelling "Your name" on his behind, is a conceptual artwork.

I love watching how much dust the Dyson vacuum cleaner sucks up after each cleaning session.

I would like to eat a chicken wrap at the Tate Modern canteen and film myself as I have an allergic reaction.

I would like to know how many times I can write my name in one hour.

I would like to write an essay with Flávia titled "The Flower and the Tree."

I drank nine glasses of carrot juice the first day I got a new juicer and was really ill for twenty-four hours.

I would like to commission my father to create several layout designs with a marker for a commissioned poster, scan them, and use them as final artwork.

I like my hair when I have not washed it for five days.

I would like to mix together every single Heinz food product and package the result in small cans labeled as a limited edition of "everything Heinz." .